OTHER PEOPLE'S FLOWERS

Compiled
by
C. C. CRANFORD

"As one might say of me that I have only made here a collection of other people's flowers, having provided nothing of my own but the cord to bind them together."
—*Montaigne's Essays*

It has been my intention to quote correctly and give due credit to all known authors in this my collection of "Other People's Flowers"—

C. C. CRANFORD

This is a limited edition for the pleasure of
my many good friends and *is not for sale*.

1940
PRINTED BY
THE LASSITER PRESS, INC.
CHARLOTTE, N. C.

Time has a way of mellowing those things we hold most dear. Throughout the years nothing has afforded me more pleasure than collecting these choice gems from the writings of my favorite authors, philosophers, poets, and—most of all—my friends.

These have been both guide and comforter to me for so many years that I want you, my friends, to share with me the joys of reading and living with them.

You will find in this volume "nothing of my own," save my joy in compiling it, and my gratefulness to those whose contributions are contained herein.

C C Crawford

OTHER PEOPLE'S FLOWERS

HAIL AND FAREWELL

We have come to the saddest and gladdest time of the year. It's a time of memory and of hope; of retrospection and introspection; of inlook and outlook; of inventory and planning. We are standing on the brink of the past, and on the threshold of the future, and on the edge of yesterday and on the hem of tomorrow. It is a time to ponder, a time to cast up the books, to turn a new page and begin a new life. It is a time when the mind wanders amid the ruins of buried memories and dead hopes, and peers out wonderingly into the mystery and haze of the future; the bells are ringing out the old year and ringing in the new. The past is gone into the forever, beyond recall, past redemption point, and the future, like a golden gleam, lies ahead with all its hidden opportunities and its unfathomable depths.

The harvests of the old year are all gathered, and now the planting time has come; the old year, with its strivings and toils, is gone, and the new year opens and beckons you to enter its mystic gates of promise. Its pathways are untrod, the pages of its book are unopened, the notes of its song are untouched, and its days and deeds are all unborn. It lies just ahead, soon to unfold its gifts, bringing gladness or sadness, enriching or robbing the heart, disturbing or rejoicing the soul, promising or refusing its rewards.

"It's a flower unborn; a book unread;
A tree with fruit unharvested;
A path untrod; a house whose rooms
Lack yet the heart's divine perfumes;
A landscape whose wide border lies
In silent shade 'neath silent skies;
A wondrous fountain yet unsealed;
A casket with its gifts concealed—
This is the year that for you awaits
Beyond tomorrow's mystic gates."

5

May it be for you a year of simple faith, joy in service, a clear outlook and a keen vision for the duties around you.

May the spell of no sordid, selfish or unworthy motive, nor anything below the noblest, touch your life with its taint for one single moment.

May your sorrows be turned into songs, your griefs into graces, your tears and toils into triumphs, and all your life made rich and strong.

May the fretting, worrying cares be lifted on wings for flight, and the happy days of Auld Lang Syne sing in your heart again this new year.

And if you are not to be shielded from all sorrow and pain, may you be strengthened to bear them like a man when they come.

And if your pathway is not to be all easy and smooth, may you be sturdy enough to tread any way, and brave enough to follow any path that opens.

And if all hardships are not to be taken away, may the timidity and fear that robs men of strength be removed as you meet life's trials.

And if you are not to know all sunshine this new year, if the shadows creep in and the lights grow dim, may you still keep faith even in the darkness.

And if life is not always pleasant, may you still live above the fret that hurts and disturbs the even harmony of your mind, above the folly that robs you of power and cripples your efficiency, above the fear that crushes courage and destroys hope and stifles life.

"I would flood your path with sunshine;
    I would fence you from all ills;
I would crown you with all blessings,
    If I could have my will.
Aye, but human love may err, friend,
    And a power all-wise is near;
So, I only pray, God bless you,
    And God keep you through the year."

—ROBERT H. McCASLIN

STUBBED HIS TOE

Did ye ever pass a youngster 'et had been an' stubbed his toe,
An' was cryin' by th' roadside sort o' lonesome like an' slow,
A-holdin' of his dusty foot, all hard an' brown an' bare,
An' tryin' to keep fr'm his eyes th' tears that's gatherin' there?
Ye hear him sort o' sobbin' like an' snuffin' of his nose,
Ye stop an' pat him on th' head an' some way try t' ease his woes,
Ye treat him sort o' kind like, an' th' fust thing that y' know
He's up an' off an' smilin'—clean forgot he stubbed his toe,

'Long th' road o' human life ye see a fellow travelin' slow,
An' like as not ye'll find he's some poor chap that's stubbed his toe.
He was makin' swimmin' headway, but he bumped into a stone,
An' his friends kep' hurryin' onward an' they left him there alone.
He ain't sobbin' er ain't sniffin'—he's too old for tears an' cries,
But he's grievin' jest as earnest, if it only comes in sighs;
An' it does a heap o' good sometimes, to go a little slow,
To say a word o' comfort to th' man that's stubbed his toe.

Ye're never sure yerself, an' th' ain't no earthly way t' know
Jes' when it's goin' t' come yer time t' trip an' stub yer toe;
To-day ye're smilin', happy in th' bright sun's heat an' glow,
To-morrow ye're a-shiverin' as ye're trudgin' through the snow.
Jest when ye think ye got th' world th' fastest in yer grip
Is th' very time, ye'll find, 'et ye're likeliest t' slip;
'N' it's mighty comfortin' t' have some fellow stop, I know,
An' speak t' ye an' kind o' help ye when ye've stubbed yer toe.

—JAMES W. FOLEY

VISIONS OF IMMORTALITY

To me the meanest flower that blows can give
Thoughts that do often lie too deep for tears.

—WILLIAM WORDSWORTH

Mr. C. C. Cranford,

Dear Neighbor and Friend:

"Every Ground-hog has his day", and *this* is *yours*, so I offer my
hearty congratulations and very best wishes for many happy returns
of your birthday; I trust you may be spared many years to your
family and church and community.   May your busy and useful life
continue to benefit your town in all lines of endeavor!   And may
you realize the approval of God in all you do!

Very sincerely your friend,

Mary H. Moring.

Asheboro, N. C.
February 2, 1930.

THE BELLS OF ST. MARY'S

The bells of St. Mary's, ah! hear, they are calling
The young loves, the true loves, who come from the sea,
And so, my beloved, when red leaves are falling,
The love-bells shall ring out—ring out for you and me.

—ANONYMOUS

THE CALL

Did you ever have a longin' to get out and buck the trail,
And to face the crashin' lightnin' and the thunder and the
    gale?
Not for no partic'lar reason but to give the world the
    laugh,
And to show the roarin' elyments you still can stand the
    gaff.

Don't you ever feel a yearnin' just to try your luck again
Down the rippin' plungin' rapids with a bunch of reg'lar
    men?
Don't you ever sorta hanker for a rough and risky trip,
Just to prove you're still a livin' and you haven't lost
    your grip?

Can't you hear the woods a-callin' for to have another try,
Sleepin' out beneath the spruces with a roof of moonlit
    sky,
With the wind a sorta singin' through the branches over-
    head
And your fire a gaily crackin' and your pipe a-glowin' red?

Don't you often get to feelin' sorta cramped and useless
    there,
Makin' figgers and a-shinin' your pants upon a chair?
Don't you yearn to get acquainted once again with Life
    and God?
If you don't, then Heaven help you, for you're dyin' in
    yer pod.

—EARL H. EMMONS

IF I WERE BOSS

If I were boss I would like to say;
"You did a good job here yesterday."
I'd look for a man, or a girl, or boy
Whose heart would leap with a thrill of joy
At a word of praise, and I'd pass it out
Where the crowd could hear as I walked about.

If I were the boss I would like to find
The fellow whose work is the proper kind;
And whenever to me a good thing came,
I'd ask to be told the toiler's name,
And I'd go to him, and I'd pat his back,
And I'd say: "That was perfectly splendid, Jack;"

Now a bit of praise isn't much to give,
But it's dear to the hearts of all who live;
And there's never a man on this good old earth
But is glad to be told that he's been of worth;
And a kindly word when the work is fair,
Is welcomed and wanted everywhere.

If I were a boss, I am sure I should
Say a kindly word whenever I could;
For the man who has given his best by day
Wants a little more than his weekly pay;
He likes to know, with the setting sun,
That his boss is pleased with the work he's done.

—EDGAR A. GUEST

INTOLERANCE

Across the way my neighbor's windows shine,
His roof-tree shields him from the storms that frown,
He toiled and saved to build it, staunch and brown,
And though my neighbor's house is not like mine,
I would not pull it down!

With patient care my neighbor, too, had built
A house of faith wherein his soul might stay,
A haven from the winds that sweep life's way.
It differed from my own—I felt no guilt—
I burned it yesterday.

—MOLLY ANDERSON HALEY

SLIPPERS

When I was young
    And my slippers were red,
I could kick higher
    Than my own head.

When I grew up
    And my slippers were white,
I could dance the stars
    Right out of the night.

Now I am old
    My slippers are black;
I walk to the corner
    And I walk back.

—ETHEL ROMIG FULLER

GOOD RULES FOR BUSINESS MEN

Don't worry; don't overbuy; don't go security.
Keep your vitality up; keep insured; keep sober; keep cool;
Stick to chosen pursuits, but not to chosen methods.
Be content with small beginnings and develop them.
Be wary of dealing with unsuccessful men.
Be cautious, but when a bargain is made stick to it.

Keep down expenses, but don't be stingy.
Make friends, but not favorites.
Don't take new risks to retrieve old losses.
Stop a bad account at once.
Make plans ahead, but don't make them in cast iron.
Don't tell what you are going to do until you have done it.

AFTER A LITTLE GIRL HAS GONE
TO SCHOOL

Because I love you, all day long
I hear the gladness of your song.
And loving you, these things I prize
The most—your smile and happy eyes.

Because I love you, I can see
All day the kiss you waved to me.
And loving you, my prayer is this:
For you some day, your daughter's kiss.

—REVAH SUMMERSGILL

Speak gently of the erring, Oh, do not thou forget,
However, deeply stained by *sin*, he is thy brother yet!
Heir of the self same heritage, child of the self same God,
He has but stumbled in the path, thou hast in weakness trod.

—LEE

NEW YEAR'S EVE

It's cruel cold on the water-front, silent and
    dark and drear;
Only the black tide weltering, only the hissing
    snow;
And I, alone, like a storm-tossed wreck, on this
    night of the glad New Year,
Shuffling along in the icy wind, ghastly and
    gaunt and slow.

They're playing a tune in McGuffy's saloon, and
    it's cheery and bright in there
(God! but I'm weak—since the bitter dawn,
    and never a bite of food);
I'll just go over and slip inside—I mustn't give
    way to despair—
Perhaps I can bum a little booze if the boys
    are feeling good.

They'll jeer at me, and they'll sneer at me, and
    they'll call me a whiskey soak;
("Have a drink? Well, thankee kindly, sir,
    I don't mind if I do.")
A drivelling, dirty, gin-joint fiend, the butt of the
    bar-room joke;
Sunk and sodden and hopeless—"Another?
    Well, here's to you!"

McGuffy is showing a bunch of the boys how
    Bob Fitsimmons hit;
The barman is talking of Tammany Hall,
    and why the ward boss got fired.
I'll just sneak into a corner and they'll let me
    alone a bit;
The room is reeling round and round. . . .
    O God! but I'm tired, I'm tired. . . .

Roses she wore on her breast that night.   Oh,
    but their scent was sweet!
Alone we sat on the balcony, and the fan-palms
    arched above;
The witching strain of a waltz by Strauss came
    up to our cool retreat,
And I prisoned her little hand in mine, and
    I whispered my plea of love.

Then sudden the laughter died on her lips, and
    lowly she bent her head;
And oh, there came in the deep, dark eyes a
    look that was heaven to see;
And the moments went, and I waited there, and
    never a word was said,
And she plucked from her bosom a rose of red
    and shyly gave it to me.

Then the music swelled to a crash of joy, and
    the lights blazed up like day,
And I held her fast to my throbbing heart,
    and I kissed her bonny brow.
"She is mine, she is mine for evermore!" the
    violins seemed to say,
And the bells were ringing the New Year in
    —O God! I can hear them now.

Don't you remember that long, last waltz, with
    its sobbing, sad refrain?
Don't you remember that last good-by, and
    the dear eyes dim with tears?
Don't you remember that golden dream, with
    never a hint of pain.
Of lives that would blend like an angel-song
    in the bliss of the coming years?

Oh, what have I lost! What have I lost!
   Ethel, forgive, forgive!
The red, red rose is faded now, and it's fifty years ago.
'Twere better to die a thousand deaths than live
   each day as I live!
I have sinned, I have sunk to the lowest
   depths—but oh, I have suffered so!
Hark! Oh, hark! I can hear the bells!
   Look! I can see her there,
Fair as a dream . . . but it fades. . . . And
   now—I can hear the dreadful hum
Of the crowded court. . . . See! the Judge looks
   down. . . . NOT GUILTY, my Lord, I swear. . . .
The bells—I can hear the bells again! . . .
   Ethel, I come, I come! . . .

* * * * * * *

"Rouse up, old man, it's twelve o'clock. You
   can't sleep here, you know.
Say! ain't you got no sentiment? Lift up
   your muddled head;
Have a drink to the glad New Year, a drop
   before you go—
You darned old dirty hobo. . . . My God!
   Here, boys! He's DEAD!"

—ROBERT SERVICE

AND WHY NOT

A full-blooded Pima Indian out in Arizona needed some cash, so he went to a banker and asked about a loan.

"How much money do you need?" asked the banker.

"Me want two hundred dollars."

"For how long?"

"Maybe two week; maybe two month."

"And what security have you?"

"Me got two hundred horses."

This seemed sufficient security, and the loan was made. A short time afterward, the Indian came into the bank with two thousand two hundred dollars cash, paid off the note and started to leave with the rest of his roll.

"Why not let us take care of that money for you?"

The old Indian's mind flew back to the day when he wanted two hundred dollars, and looking the banker straight in the eyes, he solemnly asked, "How many horses you got?"

—ANONYMOUS

———

How strangely men act! They will not praise those who are living at the same time and living with themselves; but to be themselves praised by posterity by those whom they have never seen, nor will ever see, this they set much value on.

—ANTONINUS

BEAUTY NOT WANTED

I have no use for handsome men,
　　They primp, they strut, they pose.
I'd rather love an ugly man
　　With three warts on his nose!

The homely duckling makes the best
　　Meat filling for a pie,
For it grew fat by staying home
　　Nor craved to run and fly.

The red bird and proud peacock
　　Are wonderful to see,
But yet, the homely duckling-bird
　　Is good enough for me.

The handsome man with deep-set eyes,
　　And hair that runs in curls,
Will not resist the warm impulse
　　To wink at other girls.

A handsome man?　A pretty bird?
　　They whip me into rage!
For both, in order to be kept,
　　Must be inside a cage.

—Rosa Zagnoni Marimoni

The night has a thousand eyes,
　　And the day but one;
Yet the light of the bright world dies
　　With the dying sun.
The mind has a thousand eyes,
　　And the heart but one;
Yet the light of the whole life dies
　　When love is done.

—Francis William Bourdillon

H O M E

It takes a heap o' livin' in a house t' make it home,

    A heap o' sun an' shadder, an' ye sometimes have t' roam

Afore ye really 'preciate the things ye lef' behind,

    An' hunger fer 'em somehow, with 'em allus on yer mind.

It don't make any difference how rich ye get t' be,

    How much yer chairs an' tables cost, how great yer luxury;

It ain't home t' ye, though it be the palace of a king,

    Until somehow yer soul is sort o' wrapped round everything.

Home ain't a place that gold can buy or get up in a minute;

    Afore it's home there's got to be a heap o' livin' in it;

Within the walls there's got to be some babies born, and then

    Right there ye've got t' bring 'em up t' women good, an' men;

And gradjerly, as time goes on, ye find ye wouldn't part

    With anything they ever used—they've grown into yer heart;

The old high chairs, the playthings, too, the little shoes they wore

    Ye hoard; an' if ye could ye'd keep the thumbmarks on the door.

Ye've got to weep to make it home, ye've got to sit an'
    sigh,

 An' watch beside a loved one's bed, an' know that
  Death is nigh;

An' in the stillness o'er the night t' see Death's angel come,

 An' close the eyes o' her that smiled, an' leave her
  sweet voice dumb.

Fer these are scenes that grip the heart an' when yer
    tears are dried,

Ye find the home is dearer than it was, an' sanctified;

 An' tuggin' at ye always are the pleasant memories

O' her that was an' is no more—ye can't escape from
    these.

Ye've got t' sing an' dance fer years, ye've got t' romp
    an' play,

 An' learn t' love the things ye have by usin' 'em each
  day;

Even the roses 'round the porch must blossom year by year

 Afore they 'come a part o' ye, suggestin' someone dear

Who used t' love 'em long ago, an' trained 'em jes' t'
    run

 The way they do, so's they would get the early mornin'
  sun;

Ye've got t' love each brick an' stone from cellar up to
    dome:

 It takes a heap o' livin' in a house t' make it home.

—EDGAR A. GUEST

TEN BUSINESS COMMANDMENTS

1. Don't wait for the other fellow to come to you; go to him.

2. In competition with others, always give them the credit of being a little smarter than you are. Then work like the deuce to prove they are not.

3. If you have no money and little credit, capitalize your personality. Sometimes it pays to have a nerve.

4. Never admit to anybody—and least of all to yourself—that you are licked.

5. Keep your business troubles to yourself. Nobody likes a calamity howler—besides, he finds scant favor with the bankers.

6. Don't be afraid of dreaming too big dreams. It won't hurt you to figure on owning a railroad, even if you have to compromise on a flivver.

7. Make friends; but remember that the best friends will wear out if you use them too frequently.

8. Be square even to the point of finickiness, and you will have mighty little occasion to complain of a crooked world.

9. Take advice but do your own deciding.

10. Don't toady. The world respects the man who stands on his own legs and looks it in the eye.

—ANONYMOUS

Careless seems the great avenger; history's pages but record,
Our death grapple in the darkness 'twixt old systems and the word;
Truth forever on the scaffold, wrong forever on the throne—
But the scaffold sways the future, and behind the dim unknown,
Standeth God within the shadow, keeping watch above his own.

—ANONYMOUS

IN DEFENSE OF NELLIE

Eatin' her head off, is she?
   Too old to be any good?
If you was me you'd sell her?
   Mebbe you would!

Mebbe your way is business;
   That's nuther here nor there;
I ain't talkin' business—
   That's my mare!

When I bought this place I got 'er;
   She helped me to clear this land;
And she carried me to see your mother. . .
   D'ye understand?

And I'm never gonna sell 'er,
   Nor either give 'er away;
And she'll get her oats, young feller,
   Twice a day.

          —UNKNOWN

WHAT A WOMAN CAN DO

"What can a woman do?

"She can say 'No,' and stick to it for all time.   She can also say 'No,' in such a low, soft voice that it means 'Yes.'

"She can sharpen a lead pencil, if you give her plenty of time, and plenty of pencils.

"She can dance all night in a pair of shoes two sizes too small for her, and enjoy every minute of the time."

          —ANONYMOUS

HEROISM

Of all the battles won
    The greatest is to hold
A squalling baby in your arms
    And laugh instead of scold.

—RUTHELE NOVAK

The employer questions the boy applicant for a job:

"I suppose you are a hard worker. What time do you get up in the morning?"

"Oh, I get up at half past five and have my breakfast."

"Anybody else get up at that time?"

"Oh, yes. My mother. She gets my breakfast, and then she gets dad's at half past six."

"And your dinner?"

"Oh, mother gets that, too, and then she gets father's."

"Has she the afternoon to herself?"

"Oh, no. She cleans up, looks after the children, and gets supper for dad and me when we come home. Then we get our smoke, and then we go to bed."

"And your mother?"

"Well, she does a bit of sewing then, when all is cleaned up after supper."

"What wages do you get?"

"Eighteen dollars, and dad gets thirty-five."

"And your mother?"

"What do you mean?"

"What wages does she get?"

"Oh, mother? Why, she don't get no wages. She don't work!"

—ANONYMOUS

THE LAND OF BEGINNING AGAIN

I wish that there were some wonderful place
    Called the Land of Beginning Again,
Where all our mistakes and all our heartaches,
And all our poor, selfish grief,
Could be dropped, like a shabby old coat at the door,
    And never put on again.

I wish we could come on it all unaware,
    Like the hunter who finds a lost trail,
And I wish that the one whom our blindness had done
The greatest injustice of all
Could be at the gates, like an old friend that waits
    For the comrade he's gladdest to hail.

We would all find the things we intended to do,
    But forgot, and remembered too late,
Little praises unspoken, little promises broken,
And all the thousand and one
Little duties neglected, that might have perfected
    The day for one less fortunate.

It wouldn't be possible not to be kind
    In the Land of Beginning Again;
And the ones we misjudged, and the ones whom we grudged
Their moments of victory here,
Would find in the grasp of our loving handclasp
    More than penitent lips could explain.

For what had been hardest we'd know had been best,
    And what had seemed loss would be gain;
For there is not a sting that will not take wing,
When we've faced it and laughed it away;
And I think that the laughter is most what we're after,
    In the Land of Beginning Again.

So I wish that there were some wonderful place
    Called that Land of Beginning Again,
Where all our mistakes and all our heartaches,
And all our poor, selfish grief,
Could be dropped like a shabby old coat at the door,
    And never put on again.

                —LOUISA FLETCHER

OLD MEN

I love to sit with old men
Who never speak a word;
But seem to hear the silence
That I have never heard.

They sit and look with quiet eyes
As from an evening hill
That overlooks a valley which
The distance has struck still.

I love to sit with old men
Who never say a word:
I find I rise the quieter
For Silence I've heard.

—ROBERT BELL

IN MY YARD

In my yard there are no posies rare,
Nor soft green grass growing anywhere;
It is the homeliest yard upon the street
Yet in my yard, the children always meet.
When day is done I love to hear them say,
"Gee! we've had a good time in your yard to-day."
So I keep my yard for children, and let the posies grow
In the yards where children are not allowed to go.
Some day I may live upon a childless street,
And my yard will be both prim, and neat;
But my heart—it will grow old
And only mem'ry's will my day dreams hold—
Mem'ry's of when my yard was homliest on the street,
The dear old, bare old yard, where the children used
    to meet.

—ELLA ALLEN

FROM FATHER TO SON

My son, remember you have to work. Whether you handle pick or wheelbarrow, or a set of books, dig ditches or edit a newspaper, ring an auction bell or write funny things, you must work.

Don't be afraid of killing yourself by overworking on the sunny side of thirty. Men die sometimes, but it is because they quit at 6 p.m. and don't go home until 2 a.m. It's the intervals that kill, my son. The work gives you appetite for your meals; it lends solitude to your slumber; it gives you a perfect appreciation of a holiday.

There are young men who do not work, but the country is not proud of them. It does not even know their names; it only speaks of them as "old So-and-So's boys." Nobody likes them; the great, busy world doesn't know they are here.

So find out what you want to be and do. Take off your coat and make dust in the world. The busier you are, the less harm you are apt to get into, the sweeter will be your sleep, the brighter your holidays, and the better satisfied the whole world will be with you.

—BOB BURDETTE

TO-NIGHT I WALK WITH YOU

To-night I walk with you. . .
Altho you died
My own footsteps are measured
By your stride. . .

A thousand times
We must have walked just so—
Your shoulder high,
And mine a little low. . .

To-night I walk with you. . .
Altho you died
My own footsteps are measured
By your stride. . .

—QUEENE B. LISTER

THE LAND OF PRETTY SOON

I know of a land where the streets are paved
   With the things we meant to achieve.
It is walled with the money we meant to have saved,
   And the pleasures for which we grieve.

The kind words unspoken, the promises broken
   And many a coveted boon,
Are stored away there in that land somewhere
   The land of Pretty Soon.

There are uncut jewels of a possible fame
   Lying about in the dust,
And many a noble and lofty aim
   Covered with mold and rust.

And oh, this land, though it seems so near,
   Is farther away than the moon,
Though our purpose is fair, we never get there,
   The land of Pretty Soon.

—SELECTED

THE ONLY CURE

If you don't feel just right,
If you can't sleep at night,
If you moan and you sigh,
And your throat feels dry,
If you don't care to smoke,
If your food makes you choke,
If your heart doesn't beat,
If you're getting cold feet,
If your head's in a whirl—
Why not marry the girl?

—UNKNOWN

PEACE ON EARTH, GOOD WILL TOWARD MEN!

(The Muse of A Traveling Man)

Sometimes I think that wars might cease
    If everybody, everywhere,
Could have the gift the Prince of Peace
    Intended everyone to share;
So, as I go my humble way,
I love to gain a friend each day,
And help build friendships, here and there,
Among my friends, and yours and theirs,
And maybe, some day we can fill
This grand old world with God's "Good Will."

Good Will is something folks can waste,
    Yet every day gain more and more,
For all we give is soon replaced
    With more than all we had before;
So you and I—our friends and theirs,
Can give so freely of our shares
At Christmas time—and all the year—
We might make folks so friendly here
They'll banish war some day and fill
This whole wide world with real "Good Will."

Of course, we'll never banish wars
    Till we subdue the tyrant's might,
But every soul beneath the stars
    Can help to carry on the fight
To make this world a better place,
And end forever war's disgrace;
For friendly folks, like you and me,
Or even those across the sea,
Will never feel like fighting when
We really have "Good Will Toward Men."

So let us pray that, some sweet day,
The world will learn the better way,
And we can all rejoice again
In "Peace On Earth, Good Will Toward Men."

                          —C. A. SNODGRASS

FRIENDSHIP

Some folks, we like, because we do,
Just kind o' like 'em through and through,
And as for me, It's hard to say,
Exactly, why it is this way,
And yet, it is, as I have found,
In fifty years o' knockin' 'round,
A fact that's true as true can be,
And that's the thing that puzzles me.

I can't explain, I can't define
That "something" in some friends o' mine
That seems, in sorrow, to impart
The resolution in my heart
To battle on, despite my care,
And see the sunshine everywhere,
And view the morning with its light
When everything is dark as night.

That "something" I can lean upon
In darkened hours when hope is gone;
The thing that cheers me on my way
When clouds are low and skies are gray;
That gives me hope and quiets fear,
And makes my life worth living here,
That gives of all that I may yearn,
A gift that I can ne'er return.

And should I ask, what is it, then,
That comes to me from hearts of men—
This wondrous thing I can't explain
That dries my tears and eases pain,
That makes me like 'em through and through,
And yet, not knowing why I do?
One word explains it mighty fine—
It's "friendship" true and genuine.

—FRANK CARLETON NELSON

BEYOND THE PROFIT OF TODAY

Lord, give me vision that shall see
    Beyond the profit of today
Into the years which are to be,
    That I may take the larger way
Of labor and achievement; so
    Help me fashion, staunch and sure,
A work my fellow men shall know
    As wrought to serve—and to endure.

I seek for fortune, Lord, nor claim
    To scorn the recompense I earn;
But help me, as I play the game,
    To give the world its just return.
Thou mad'st the earth for all of us,
    Teach me through struggle, strain and stress
To win and do my share, for thus
    Can profit lead to happiness.

Guard me from thoughts of little men
    Which blind the soul to greater things;
Save me from smug content and then
    From greed and selfishness it brings;
Aid me to join that splendid clan
    Of Business Men who seek to trace
A calm, considered working-plan
    To make the world a better place.

Lord, let the faith of these be mine,
    A creed creative, simple, true,
Let me but aid in their design,
    Let me but share the work they do;
Teach me to hold this task above
    All lesser thoughts within my ken,
That thus I may be worthy of
    The name of Business Man; Amen!

—ANONYMOUS

YESTERDAY

What a day, was yesterday,
For yesterday gave me, you,
All my schemes, and golden dreams,
At last it seems have come true.
Until I found you the skies were always gray,
Then like the sunshine you drove the clouds away.
You'll never guess, My happiness,
When you said yes, yesterday.

—COPYRIGHT, TED BROWNE MUSIC CO., INC.

Persistency is characteristic of all men who have accomplished anything great. They may lack in some other particular, may have many weaknesses and eccentricities, but the quality of persistence is never absent in a successful man. No matter what opposition he meets, or what discouragements overtake him, he is always persistent. Drudgery cannot disgust him, labour cannot weary him. He will persist, no matter what comes or what goes; it is a part of his nature; he could almost as easily stop breathing. It is not so much brilliancy of intellect or fertility of resource as persistency of effort, constancy of purpose, that gives success. Persistency always inspires confidence. Everybody believes in the man who persists. He may meet misfortunes, sorrows, and reverses, but everybody believes that he will ultimately triumph, because they know there is no keeping him down. "Does he keep at it—is he persistent?" This is the question which the world asks about a man. Even a man with small ability will often succeed if he has the quality of persistency, where a genius without it would fail.

"You ask me how it is I have done what you call so much in the way of exploring. If, for a moment, I accept your estimate of my achievements, it is only in order that I may emphasize one article of my faith. That is that nothing in the world is difficult if people will only go about it in the right way. The only reason, I think, why people do not do things is because they are afraid. There are two words which, when exploring, are not, and never have been in my vocabulary; they are 'but and if.' If a man will only eliminate them from his life he can do practically anything he wishes."

—HENRY SAVAGE LANDOR

ME AND JOE

Up in the attic near the sky
Where we used to sleep in the days gone by!
Oh, the dreams we dreamed and the tales we told
When the winds were wild and the nights were cold;
And the things we planned and the trips we took
And the fish we caught with line and hook—
Up in the attic where me and Joe
Used to sleep in the long ago!

Oh, the scuffles and frolics and toe-nail fights
And the dogs that howled in the winter nights!
How "skeered" we'd get when the lamps were out
At the big black things that stood about;
What awful forms in the room we saw
And how we'd "holler" for paw and maw—
Up in the attic where me and Joe
Used to sleep in the long ago!

And the bees that came at the dawn of Spring
To the apple trees where the birds would sing;
The katydids and the cricket's call
And the ivy that scratched on the attic wall;
And the mellow light of the moon that shed
Its gentle beams across our bed—
Up in the attic where me and Joe
Used to sleep in the long ago!

Oh, the face will wrinkle and hair turn gray
And dim grow the road to yesterday;
The throat will choke and the tears will start
And something pull at the aching heart
When Memory thrums at the pulsing string
And a voice comes back and sighs and sings
Of the dear old attic where me and Joe
Used to sleep in the long ago!

—BRODIE PAYNE

FORGET IT

If you see a tall fellow ahead of the crowd
    A leader of men marching fearless and proud,
And you know of a tale, whose mere telling aloud
    Would cause his proud head in anguish be bowed,
It's a pretty good plan to forget it.

If you know of a skeleton hidden away
    In a closet, and guarded, and kept from the way
In the dark, and whose showing, sudden display
    Would cause grief and sorrow and life-long dismay,
It's a pretty good plan to forget it.

If you know of a thing that would darken the joy
    Of a man or a woman, a girl or a boy,
That will wipe out a smile, or the least bit annoy,
    It's a pretty good plan to forget it.

—ANONYMOUS

TO THE WOMAN I MARRIED

We cannot say, "We've never had a word,"
    For we are pretty human, you and I.
Some arguments of yours I thought absurd,
    And, manlike, told you; and it made you cry.

We've disagreed along some minor things,
    And I still think I'm right in not a few,
I must confess we've neither sprouted wings—
    But we have Faith, which I will take in lieu.

And we have loyalty, that made the years
    A path to Arcady for lovers' feet.
And oh, what laughter followed all our tears!
    And we have shared—and sharing was so sweet!

—ROSCOE GILMORE STOTT

OCTOBER

October, with a lavish hand, now spills
Her wine of flame and gold upon the hills;
It splashes on the slopes and blends into
Rich coloring of almost every hue:
Deep red and russet, orange, yellow, jade,
Grape-blue and green and brown of every shade.
And in the valley hang, like flimsy mist,
Her veils of opal, blue, and amethyst,
Rose-gray and violet, until it seems
All earth is drowsy with the wine of dreams.
I think that somewhere up around the Throne
God's cup of glory must have overflown.

—JAMES COURTNEY CHALLIS

INVINCTUS

Out of the night that covers me,
    Black as the pit from pole to pole,
I thank whatever gods may be
    For my unconquerable soul.
In the fell clutch of circumstance,
    I have not winced nor cried aloud.
Under the bludgeonings of chance
    My head is bloody, but unbowed,
Beyond this place of wrath and tears
    Looms but the horror and the shade,
And yet the menace of the years
    Finds, and shall find me, unafraid.
It matters not how strait the gate,
    How charged with punishment the scroll,
I am the Master of my fate;
    I am the captain of my soul.

—WILLIAM ERNEST HENLEY

STUNG

The deeds of hornet, wasp and bee,
  Are often widely sung;
But the saddest wail from lips of men,
  Is the wail that says, "I'm stung."

Oh, the honey bee has a red hot foot,
  The wasp has a slender tail,
And the bumblebee sits down quite hard,
  While the hornet turns you pale.

The sting of the bee is hard to bear,
  It makes you ache and fret,
But the sting that's made by a trusted friend
  Is the one you don't forget.

—HARRY BROKAW

For three hours he had hung there.
He now felt the sleep of death creeping into his veins—
His head drooped forward.
Below he saw the soldiers;
All around surged the waiting mob, watching his death struggles.
He aroused himself and prayed,
"Father, forgive them for they know not what they do!"
Another unconscious struggle—
Nature trying to gain her freedom!
Again he spoke—
"Father, into thy hands I commend my spirit!"

That proud head fell forward.
The form relaxed, swayed and hung limp and still upon the cross.
A soldier with a spear pierced his side, but there was no response
  of life.
Death, in pity, had set the captive free.

Only a thorn-crowned, bleeding Christ could have won the adoration
  of a world.

—ELBERT HUBBARD
in The Man of Sorrows

REMEMBER

Remember me when I am gone away,
Gone far away into the silent land,
When you can no more hold me by the hand,
Nor I half turn to go, yet turning stay.
Remember me when no more day by day
You tell me of our future that you plann'd;
Only remember me; you understand
It will be late to counsel then or pray.
Yet if you should forget me for a while
And afterwards remember, do not grieve;
For if the darkness and corruption leave
A vestige of the thoughts that once I had
Better by far you should forget and smile
Than that you should remember and be sad.

—CHRISTINA G. ROSSETTI

HUSBANDS

A husband is a useless thing;
    He sits around and smokes;
And when a wife is serious—
    Why that's the time he jokes;
But when his wife is playful
    And wants to see the town,
Why then he grabs a paper
    And promptly sits him down.

A husband is a cussed male
    Inclined a bit to fuss
When things are very peaceful;
    The first to make a muss
When everything is tidy;
    And yet I'm frank to say
A wife is strangely lonesome
    When the dear old brute's away!

—ROSCOE GILMORE STOTT

WAKE UP!

"Most people resist waking up. They yawn, turn over, cover up, and try to stay asleep. No matter what the hour, they are not quite ready to wake up. They look daggers at the alarm clock, and curse the sun for shining in through the window. And yet, waking up is a precious experience. There's nothing else like it. To come out of darkness into light! Out of dormancy into consciousness! Out of inertia into activity!

"Everybody should look forward to waking up—not only out of sleep, but out of ignorance, bad habits, laziness, discouragement and many et ceteras.

"Such awakening can take place all day long—every day.

"Don't resist it with a yawn. Don't turn away from it. And don't try to cover up.

"Be ready for it. Be willing to learn—to be active—to go ahead—and to be a credit to those who care for you."

—ANONYMOUS

THE OFFICE PESSIMIST

They called him Pessimistic Dan,
    A most peculiar sort of man—
The kind that people talk about,
    But even then I had a doubt
That Dan could be so full of gloom,
    Until I stopped off at his room
And saw perched there in open view—
    Alarm clocks! no, not one—but two!
He would not trust in one alone,
    He told me in his mournful tone,
And even then, I tried to be
    Forgiving—but he puzzled me.
The thing that really changed my mind,
    Was not the words of folks unkind—
But how convinced I finally felt—
    He wore suspenders and a belt!

—ROBERT W. KERNAGHAN

THE SHOOTING OF DAN McGREW

A bunch of the boys were whooping it up in the
  Malamute saloon;
The kid that handles the music-box was hitting
  a jag-time tune;
Back of the bar, in a solo game, sat Dangerous
  Dan McGrew,
And watching his luck was his light-o'-love, the
  lady that's known as Lou.

When out of the night, which was fifty below,
  and into the din and the glare,
There stumbled a miner fresh from the creeks,
  dog-dirty, and loaded for bear,
He looked like a man with a foot in the grave
  and scarcely the strength of a louse,
Yet he tilted a poke of dust on the bar, and he
  called for drinks for the house.
There was none could place the stranger's face,
  though we searched ourselves for a clue;
But we drank to his health, and the last to drink
  was Dangerous Dan McGrew.

There's men that somehow just grip your eyes,
  and hold them hard like a spell;
And such was he, and he looked to me like a
  man who had lived in hell;
With a face most hair, and the dreary stare of
  a dog whose day is done,
As he watered the green stuff in his glass, and
  the drops fell one by one.

Then I got to figgering who he was, and wondering
    what he'd do,
And I turned my head—and there watching
    him was the lady that's known as Lou.

His eyes went rubbering round the room, and
    he seemed in a kind of daze,
Till at last that old piano fell in the way of his
    wandering gaze.
The rag-time kid was having a drink; there
    was no one else on the stool,
So the stranger stumbles across the room, and
    slops down there like a fool.
In a buckskin shirt that was glazed with dirt
    he sat, and I saw him sway;
Then he clutched the keys with his talon hands
    —my God! but that man could play.

Were you ever out in the Great Alone, when the
    moon was awful clear,
And the icy mountains hemmed you in with a
    silence you most could hear;
With only the howl of a timber wolf, and you
    camped there in the cold,
A half-dead thing in a stark, dead world, clean
    mad for the muck called gold;
While high overhead, green, yellow and red,
    the North Lights swept in bars?—
Then you've a haunch what the music meant
    . . . hunger and night and the stars.

And hunger not of the belly kind, that's banished
    with bacon and beans,
But the gnawing hunger of lonely men for a
    home and all that it means;
For a fireside far from the cares that are, four
    walls and a roof above;

But oh! so cramful of cosy joy, and crowned
    with a woman's love—
A woman dearer than all the world, and true
    as Heaven is true—
(God! how ghastly she looks through her
    rouge—the lady that's known as Lou).

Then on a sudden the music changed, so soft
    that you scarce could hear;
But you felt that your life had been looted clean
    of all that it once held dear;
That someone had stolen the woman you loved;
    that he love was a devil's lie;
That your guts were gone, and the best for you
    was to crawl away and die.
'Twas the crowning cry of a heart's despair,
    and it thrilled you through and through—
"I guess I'll make it a spread misere," said
    Dangerous Dan McGrew.

The music almost died away . . . . then it burst
    like a pent-up flood;
And it seemed to say "Repay, repay," and my
    eyes were blind with blood.
The thought came back of an ancient wrong,
    and it stung like a frozen lash,
And the lust awoke to kill, to kill . . . . then
    the music stopped with a crash,
And the stranger turned, and his eyes they
    burned in a most peculiar way;
In a buckskin shirt that was glazed with dirt
    he sat, and I saw him sway;
Then his lips went in in a kind of grin, and he
    spoke, and his voice was calm,
And "Boys," says he, "you don't know me,
    and none of you care a damn;

But I want to state, and my words are straight,
    and I'll bet my poke they're true,

That one of you is a hound of hell . . . . and
    that one is Dan McGrew."

Then I ducked my head, and the lights went
    out, and two guns blazed in the dark,

And a woman screamed, and the lights went up,
    and two men lay stiff and stark.

Pitched on his head, and pumped full of lead,
    was Dangerous Dan McGrew,

While the man from the creeks lay clutched to
    the breast of the lady that's known as Lou.

These are the simple facts of the case, and I
    guess I ought to know.

They say that the stranger was crazed with
    "hooch," and I'm not denying it's so.

I'm not so wise as the lawyer guys, but strictly
    between us two—

The woman that kissed him and—pinched his poke—
    was the lady that's known as Lou.

—ROBERT SERVICE

THE PRESENT CRISIS

Then to side with Truth is noble, when we share her wretched crust,

Ere her cause bring fame and profit, and 'tis prosperous to be just;

Then it is the brave man chooses, while the coward stands aside,

Doubting in his object spirit, till his Lord is crucified,

And the multitude make virtue of the faith they had denied.

—JAMES RUSSELL LOWELL

WHERE THE WILD FLOWERS BLOOM

In the depths of a gray old forest,
    By the side of a singing brook,
Where the moss grows green on the tree trunks,
    I know of a sheltered nook.
Afar from the strife and tumult,
    Afar from the cares of the day;
Alone to that peaceful woodland
    I wander, in silence, away.

Where the rugged rocks lie scattered,
    And the oaks in grandeur rise,
There a scene of sylvan beauty
    Brings rest to my weary eyes.
There the hand of the Master Artist
    With infinite tender care,
Hath woven a magic carpet
    Of the woodland flowers so fair.

Then I watch as they nod in the breezes,
    While I stand at the foot of a tree
And their spell, like a radiant vision,
    Doth furnish enchantment for me.
Oh, the flowers that bloom in the Maytime,
    Far off in a wooded glen,
When we seek them alone in the shadows,
    Will solace the cares of men.

—HARRY BROKAW

I sit a patient cat at the rat hole of my character for twenty-three hours. At the twenty-fourth a rat escapes. That escape and not my watchfulness is the measure of my character.

—CLIFFORD RAYMOND

JEST 'FORE CHRISTMAS

Father calls me William, sister calls me Will,
Mother calls me Willie, but the fellers call me Bill!
Mighty glad I ain't a girl—ruther be a boy,
Without them sashes, curls, an' things that's worn by Fauntleroy!
Love to chawnk green apples an' go swimmin' in the lake—
Hate to take the castor-ile they give for belly-ache!
'Most all the time, the whole year round, there ain't no flies on me,
But jest 'fore Christmas I'm as good as I can be!

Got a yeller dog named Sport, sick him on the cat;
First thing she knows she doesn't know where she is at!
Got a clipper sled, an' when us kids goes out to slide,
'Long comes the grocery cart, an' we all hook a ride!
But sometimes when the grocery man is worrited an' cross,
He reaches at us with his whip, an' larrups up his hoss,
An' then I laff an' holler, "Oh, ye never teched me!"
But jest 'fore Christmas I'm as good as I kin be!

Gran'ma says she hopes that when I git to be a man,
I'll be a missionarer like her oldest brother Dan,
As was et up by the cannibals that live in Ceylon's Isle,
Where every prospeck pleases, an' only man is vile!
But gran'ma she has never been to see a Wild West show,
Nor read the life of Daniel Boone, or else I guess she'd know
That Buff'lo Bill an' cowboys is good enough for me!
Excep' jest 'fore Christmas, when I'm as good as I kin be!

And then old Sport he hangs around, so solemn-like an' still,
His eyes they seem a-sayin': "What's the matter, little Bill?"
The old cat sneaks down off her perch an' wonders what's become
Of them two enemies of hern that used to make things hum!
But I am so perlite and tend so earnestly to biz,
That mother says to father: "How improved our Willie is!"
But father, havin' been a boy hisself, suspicions me
When jest 'fore Christmas, I'm as good as I kin be!

For Christmas, with its lots an' lots of candies, cakes an' toys,
Was made, they say, for proper kids an' not for naughty boys;
So wash yer face an' bresh yer hair, an' mind yer p's and q's,
And don't bust out yer pantaloons, and don't wear out yer shoes;
Say "Yessum" to the ladies, and "Yessur" to the men,
An' when they's company, don't pass yer plate for pie again;
But, thinkin' of the things yer'd like to see upon that tree,
Jest 'fore Christmas be as good as yer kin be!

—EUGENE FIELD

————

ONLY ONCE

Through this toilsome world, alas!
Once, and only once, I pass.
If a kindness I may show,
If a good deed I may do
To my suffering fellow men,
Let me do it while I can,
Nor delay it; for 'tis plain
I shall not pass this way again.

—JOSEPH A. TORREY

WAITING

Serene, I fold my hands and wait,
   Nor care for wind, or tide, or sea;
I rave no more 'gainst Time or Fate,
   For, lo! my own shall come to me.

I stay my haste, I make delays,
   For what avails this eager pace?
I stand amid the eternal ways,
   And what is mine shall know my face.

Asleep, awake, by night or day,
   The friends I seek are seeking me;
No wind can drive my bark astray,
   Nor change the tide of destiny.

What matter if I stand alone?
   I wait with joy the coming years;
My heart shall reap where it hath sown,
   And garner up its fruit of tears.

The waters know their own and draw
   The brook that springs in yonder heights;
So flows the good with equal law
   Unto the soul of pure delights.

The stars come nightly to the sky;
   The tidal wave unto the sea;
Nor time, nor space, nor deep, nor high,
   Can keep my own away from me.

—JOHN BURROUGHS

MOTHERS

Mothers are the queerest things!
   'Member when John went away
All but mother cried and cried
   When they said good-by that day.
She just talked, and seemed to be
   Not the slightest bit upset—
Was the only one who smiled!
   Others' eyes were streaming wet.

But when John came back again
   On a furlough, safe and sound,
With a medal for his deeds,
   And without a single wound,
While the rest of us hurrahed,
   Laughed and joked and danced about,
Mother kissed him, then she cried—
   Cried and cried like all git out!

—EDWIN L. SABIN

Here lies a man who saved his all
For days when rain and snow should fall;
He knew no pleasures, shared no game,
And died before the blizzard came!

—ANONYMOUS

Fair be the path beneath your feet,
   Bright be the skies above you,
Where e'r you go, still may you meet
   Friends that will truly love you.

—ANONYMOUS

A GIFT

I have so little to give, my dear,
So little of silver and gold;
But I can give you a gift, my dear,
That couldn't be bought or sold.

My friendship, if you find it sweet;
My smile of greeting, when we meet;
My tears, to comfort you in pain;
My smile, to cheer you up again;
My hand to hold, in joy or sorrow;
My love Today—My Love Tomorrow!

—CHESTA HOLT FULMER

THREE ANSWERS

"Oh, where is Love?" I asked of one
    In childhood's sunny May.
"In leafy grove, in meadow green,
    In clover-fields astray."

"Oh, where is Love?" I asked of him
    In manhood's golden prime.
"In beauty's bright, bewitching eye,
    In lips as rich as wine."

"Oh, where is Love?" I asked of Age,
    White crowned, his sands near run.
"In loyal hearts, in lives sublime,
    In souls that light us on."

—ANONYMOUS

AT THIS HOUR

There comes a time at evening, as the day begins to gloom,
    As the shades of twilight deepen and creep across the
        room
To my chair before the fire; when in its glow I see
    Far visions of my childhood, old memories dear to me;
And again I'm just a tired child now soothed and lulled to
        rest
    In gentle arms that hold me close against the loving
        breast.
    Of my Mother—at this hour.

But my reverie is broken by an eager, childish call;
    And the sound of tiny footsteps pattering softly through
        the hall
Wakens other recollections as I hurry out to greet
    My own sweet, sleepy darling toddling in on tired feet;
Oh, tenderly I cuddle her as eyelids droop and close;
    She, too, all wearied out with play, at last has sought
        repose
    With her Mother—at this hour.

Then rekindling embers brighten, and in the flames I see
    My little sleeping baby girl a woman grown to be,
And the sudden, prescient vision brings the tears into my
        eyes;
    And yet—oh, grateful solace!—'tis a blessing in disguise;
For I see her with her own sweet babe before another blaze
    Wherein she finds the loved one of her own lost yesterdays—
    Her Mother—at this hour.

                    —C. J. INGRAM

WE WANTED A GIRL

We wanted a girl with a pair of blue eyes,
With two little hands of a lovable size
To reach for a cookie—a wee, laughing miss
With pink cheeks to pat and red lips to kiss,
With hair that her mother could toy with and curl.
We knew what we wanted: we wanted a girl.

We wanted an eager face, dimpled and sweet;
And ten tiny toes on two fat little feet
To count every night, after each day of wear
That little toes get, to be sure they were there;
And baby teeth gleaming, each one like a pearl.
We wanted—and oh, how we wanted—a girl.

And now in the dusk when a little form creeps
To lie in a lap, and a little one sleeps,
Above her we bend, and in thankfulness there
Two hearts in the silence are breathing a prayer—
Two love-laden hearts that with joy are awhirl,
Two hearts overflowing. We wanted a girl!

—LARRY FLINT

TO A WATERFOWL

He who, from zone to zone,
Guides through the boundless sky thy certain flight,
In the long path that I must tread alone
Will lead my steps aright.

—WILLIAM CULLEN BRYANT

SHAKESPEARE SAID:

So much for that . . . . Better three hours too soon than a minute
too late . . . . All the fat is in the fire . . . . You egg . . . . Wild-
goose chase . . . . Too good to be so . . . . Against the grain . . . . Up
in the air . . . . Take a homely man's advice . . . . Not so hot . . . .
Let's have no more fooling about it . . . . It is neither here nor there
. . . . I'll be hanged . . . . Green-eyed jealousy . . . . Hanging is too
good . . . . He hath eaten me out of house and home . . . . Give the
devil his due . . . . Go hang yourself . . . . A hell of a time I
feel it upon my bones . . . . It is but so so . . . . Let the world slide
. . . . Too much of a good thing . . . . We have seen better days . . . .
Well said . . . . Ye gods . . . . Strike home . . . . Now or never,
sister . . . . O boy . . . . My heart into my mouth . . . . Is she so hot?
. . . . I'll never look you in the face . . . . Had I the heart to do it
. . . . Done me wrong . . . . Every inch a king . . . . Dry as hay . . . .
Care killed a cat . . . . But the point is this . . . . Apple of his eye
. . . . Hair-breadth escapes . . . . I will tell him my mind . . . . One
for all, or all for one . . . . She's too rough for me . . . . Ten to
one . . . . What the devil . . . . Have a beard grow in the palm of
my hand . . . . Every man has his fault . . . . As gentle as a lamb
. . . . Cock-sure . . . . Dead as a door nail . . . . On my word . . . .
What was it to you? . . . . You have your hands full . . . . As good
luck would have it . . . . From post to pillar . . . . I would not for a
million . . . . O! my word . . . . Poor but honest . . . . Death will
have his day . . . . Gave up the ghost . . . . Hob, nob . . . . Plucked
in the bud . . . . Rotten times . . . . True love never did run smooth
. . . . Water cannot wash away your sin . . . . Hood-wink him . . . .
As a nose on a man's face . . . . Cut one another's throat . . . . She
falls for it . . . . That it should come to this . . . . We are lucky, boy
. . . . What's in a name? . . . . Something is rotten in the state of
Denmark . . . . Talk till doomsday . . . . We'll do anything for gold
. . . . Spite of hell . . . . The sooner the better . . . . There's something

tells me . . . . What's mine is yours . . . . and what is yours is mine
. . . . So help me . . . . The fresh fish . . . . True as steel . . . . Swim
like a duck . . . . The milk of human kindness.

————

THE KNOCKERS

I know he must be doing well,
    I know he's getting on,
His work has now begun to tell,
    His struggle time has gone;
He now has passed the dreary days,
    The lonesome ones and grim,
And now is treading better ways,
    For folks are knocking him.

His skill has caught the eye of men,
    His worth is seen at last,
He's left the throng that knew him when
    His skies were overcast.
He's won the laurel for his brow
    By toil and pluck and vim;
And he is doing real work now,
    For folks are knocking him.

The knocker is a curious cuss;
    He never starts to whine
Or fling his envious shafts at us
    Until our work is fine.
It's only men with skill to do
    Real work he tries to block;
And so congratulations to
    The man the knockers knock!

—JO E. HENRY

SECONDS

All time, no matter how we may think of it, is made up of seconds, and to each one of us is given but one second to live at a time. A second is a very small stage upon which to stand, and yet our entire lives, whether happy or unhappy, successful or unsuccessful, have to be played within its limits.

Years are made up of seconds, so our lives are made up of what we do one second at a time and NOW, the present moment, is the all-important thing for our consideration, for if this second is wasted it will be lost for all time:

> Lost yesterday,
> Somewhere between Sunrise and Sunset,
> Two golden hours.
> Each set with sixty diamond minutes.
> No reward is offered,
> They are gone forever.

Some people spend their days in the past, wandering about through old experiences as one would wander about through an ancient graveyard, lamenting over the dead opportunities of the past. They have but one day in their calendar and that day is *yesterday*. Others live only in dreams and their one day in the almanac is *tomorrow*. Today is neglected and tomorrow never comes. The only successful man is the one who knows how to make good use of the present moment, no matter how dull and commonplace it may seem to him.

It is said that Napoleon lost the battle of Waterloo through one misspent second. He had been denying himself sufficient sleep and in the most critical moment of that critical battle he became drowsy. He felt that one moment of relaxation would not hurt and so yielded. During that brief spell he mumbled a false order and lost the battle. Marshal Ney tried to buy back that lost second and though he paid a tremendous price in blood and human lives, the chance of victory was lost forever.

A lot can be done in one second of time. The sunlight travels 186,000 miles in a second, and the electric current goes more than 7 times around the world in that same short space of time. A photographer in an airplane needs only the smallest fraction of a second to take a perfect picture of a vast landscape with forests, fields of grain, and clustering villages.

The brain of a healthy individual thinks with the same rapidity, and, if he has been careful of the former seconds, and trained his brain to think truthfully and honestly, he can, in one second forecast the future and make decisions that will tell throughout his life.

Alexander-the-Great was asked the secret of his skill in conquering a world and he replied: "By not wavering." He made good use of a second and changed all history.

One of America's great generals (Grant) said: "There comes always in a close battle a critical moment when both armies have done their best up to their natural endurance. Each is trembling and uncertain—at the limit, anxious to see what will come next. At that second, to strike first and hard is to win."

Stonewall Jackson stands as one of the great, out-standing generals of all time. No man ever covered so many miles with his army, fought so many battles, and won so many victories in so short a time, and the reason was—he never lost a second.

To waver in the right use of the present moment is to lose the battle and an opportunity lost is lost forever.

To succeed is to be able to make instant choice and as quickly sacrifice every conflicting plan and purpose.

There was a second when Jefferson thought out the Declaration of Independence, and in that second that he decided to write it— a nation bgan to be born.

There was a second when Washington first conceived of crossing the Delaware that Christmas time, and in that second the victorious end of the Revolutionary War came in sight.

There was a second in mid-ocean, when ice began to form on the wings of his plane that Lindbergh made a quick decision, saved himself from a watery grave, and gave life to Aviation.

It is the quick, alert mind that sees the value of an immediate decision, and realizes that no better time will ever come, that this second is the best second of a lifetime, that wealth and fame and honor come.

A great orator (Dr. Talmage) once said: "Of all the centuries of the world this is the best century, of all the decades of a century this is the best decade, of all the years in a decade this is the best year, of all the days in a year, this is the best day, of all the hours in a day this is the best hour, of all the minutes in an hour this is the best minute, of all the seconds in a minute this is the best second."

—ANONYMOUS

I SHALL NOT FAIL

I shall not fail if you believe in me,
Though life may lead the way across a sea
Of billowing waves, of wild and fierce intent,
Of hard, steep paths that leave me bruised and spent.

I shall surmount all doubt and craven fear,
with added courage face each coming year—
No goal too great—no crest too high shall be
If only you keep faith and trust in me.

—KATHERINE EDELMAN

SONG OF COURAGE

(No matter where or how you have failed, the desire within to rise
again, is the power to help you rise.—Saying of a Sage.)

I have fallen.
But bravely I shall rise.
The road is rough and long.
Its grey dust blinds my eyes.
But I have yet a chance
To win a worthy prize.

I have fallen.
Yea, time and time again.
Still, I shall stumble on
In agony and pain.
And who will dare to say
My hope has been in vain?

I have fallen
And shattered my frail soul.
But I shall try to weld
The fragments to a whole.
Scarred, and crushed and bruised,
Thus, I shall reach the Goal.

—KATHLEEN LAMB

If I can stop one heart from breaking,
I shall not live in vain:
If I can ease one life the aching
Or cool one pain,
Or help one fainting robin
Unto his nest again,
I shall not live in vain.

—EMILY DICKINSON

CHRISTMAS EVE

The whole world pauses on this night,
    In its mad fight for gold,
To draw the bonds of love afresh
    About each separate fold.

The cares of life are thrust aside,
    The scheming brain becomes
Alert to dearer, simpler things,
    Like trumpets, dolls, and drums.

The year-old battle and its scars
    Are kept outside tonight;
They have no place beside a tree
    Aglow with tapers bright.

God pity him who cannot bring
    Upon each Christmas Eve,
An humble and contrite heart,
    Its blessings to receive.

God pity him who walks in pride,
    His soul with greed defiled,
Who will not stoop, with outstretched arms,
    To clasp a little child.

Man may not live by bread alone,
    But by good deeds which start
and shed their precious perfume from
    The flowers of the heart.

—EDWIN CARLISLE LITSEY

———

The darkest night the world has ever seen, did not put out the stars.

WORDS

Words that are bitter should never be spoken,
    Black, angry words that pierce like a dart,
For love can be blighted and friendship be broken
    By the sting and the sorrow they bring to the heart.

But even more deadly, more cruel and more fearsome
    Are words that are whispered—God shudders with pain
At the thought of the brave, noble souls that have perished—
    The innocent victims that slander has slain.

But sweet words of kindness, like jewels they glisten.
    Who can measure their worth? It is priceless indeed.
Only God can keep record of all they accomplish—
    They build the foundation for every great deed.

—KATHERINE EDELMAN

THE FISH

I'm the commonest fish in the water,
    I don't even know what's my name,
But I'm very content and happy,
    In the pond where I live, just the same.

There's a preacher lives up in the village,
    And he tells people they should be kind,
But his chiefest delight is in fishing,
    He says it unburdens his mind.

So he sits on the bank by the hour,
    And says things because we don't bite;
Were we needed for food 'twould be different,
    But to kill us for fun don't seem right.

We fish don't object to good preaching,
    That saves wayward men by the score;
But when a man's really converted,
    He won't kill for fun any more.

—FRANK T. SHEARER

THE LITTLE HOUSE

Ah, it's home, dearie, home that my heart turns to forever—
A little house, a bit o' green upon a quiet street;
White curtains at the windows, and a red bloom peering outward;
And the clicking o' the kitchen tiles to my own happy feet.

Ah, it's home, dearie, home, and the singing o' the kettle,
And a table spread at evening time a waiting there for you—
The early lamp all lighted, and the fire burning cheery—
And a soft wind blowing inward from the sweet world o' dew.

And listen, dearie, close beside, a baby in a cradle,
A-swinging low—a swinging low—(I'm singing for him, dear,)
Just a little song o' living, like the south wind to the roses—
"It's evening time, and home time, and he will soon be here."

—GRACE NOLL CROWELL

GRADATIM

Heaven is not reached at a single bound;
But we build the ladder by which we rise
From the lowly earth to the vaulted skies,
And we mount to its summit round by round.

—JOSIAH GILBERT HOLLAND

Whoever will prosper in any line of life must save his own time and do his own thinking. He must spend neither time nor money which he has not earned.

—DAVID STARR JORDAN

JOY AND SORROW

With Joy I traveled land and sea,
But Sorrow followed after me;
I tripped the sands, I sailed the tide,
With Sorrow always at my side.

When all the skies were all aflame,
My happiest moment, Sorrow came
And touched my shoulder, made me turn
Some sombre truth of life to learn.

So I have gone, the man, the boy,
By Pain accompanied, and Joy—
Whatever pleasure I would win,
No joy but had some sorrow in.

Yes, Joy has often tripped with me
The yellow sands, and sailed the sea.
Joy gave me joy, and skies a-glow—
But Sorrow taught me all I know.

—DOUGLAS MALLOCH

A PESSIMIST

The traditional attitude of the pessimist toward all things is
represented thus in a dialogue with a farmer:
"How do you like this weather?"
"Not much, I'm feared it's goin' to rain."
"Well, how's times with you?"
"Sorter so-so . . . but they won't last."
"Folks all well?"
"Yes, but the measles is in the neighborhood."
"Well, you ought to be thankful you're a-livin'."
"I reckon so; but we've all got to die!"

—ANONYMOUS

A HELPING HAND

On the lowest round of the ladder
 I firmly planted my feet,
And looked up at the dim, vast distance
 That made my future so sweet.

I climbed till my vision grew weary,
 I climbed till my brain was on fire,
I planted each footstep with wisdom—
 Yet I never seemed to get higher.

For this round was glazed with indifference,
 And that one was gilded with scorn,
And when I grasped firmly another,
 I found, under velvet, a thorn.

Till my brain grew weary of planning,
 And my heart strength began to fail,
And the flush of the morning's excitement,
 Ere evening, commenced to pale.

But just when my hands were unclasping
 Their hold on the last-gained round,
When my hopes, coming back from the future,
 Were sinking again to the ground,

One who had climbed near to the summit
 Reached backward a helping hand;
And, refreshed, encouraged and strengthened,
 I took, once again, my stand.

And I wish—oh, I wish—that the climbers
 Would never forget, as they go,
That, though weary may seem their climbing,
 There is always someone below.

        —ANONYMOUS

T O DA D

Never had much style about him, never cared for dress;
Sort o' spent his life a sowin' seeds of happiness;
Doin' little things for others, helpin' where he could;
Never makin' much pretension, always doin' good.

Home, for him, was all for livin', filled his heart with pride,
And his doors were ever open, latch strings hung outside.
Folks who came were always welcome, loved to have them round;
Wanted much of joy and laughter, seemed to love the sound.

Had his cares and had his troubles, same as all of us;
Figured them a part of livin', never made much fuss;
Made the best of all God gave him, as through life he went,
Ever toiling, giving, taking, kind and provident.

Vain, the tribute we would pay him, words cannot express
What it meant to have him with us and our thankfulness;
Sweet, the memory he has left us, though our hearts are sad;
Great the blessing that was given, just to call him Dad.

—FRANK CARLETON NELSON

HIS MAJESTY'S FISTS

Tiny, chubby, dimpled fists
    Waving through the air,
As he coos with sheer delight
    From his throne High Chair.

Now he rubs his dreamy eyes;
    Sandman must be near,
For he nods his curly head;
    Rubs one shell pink ear.

Oh! Sweet King of Babyland
    You just rule us all,
With your precious baby ways,
    And your fists so small.

—BETTIE ALLEN GREER

ULTIMATE ROSE

When I am dead
Let no one bow his head
To talk or preach or pray,
Or walk with solemn tread
Beside this clay.
When I am dead
Tears should remain unshed
That day.

When I am dead
I want a rose instead
Tender and proud and gay—
Flaming with rebel red—
To say
Softly, when I am dead,
What can be truly said
No other way.

—RALPH CHAPLIN

TEMPER

When I have lost my temper I have lost my reason, too.
I'm never proud of anything which angrily I do.
When I have talked in anger and my cheeks were flaming red,
I have always uttered something which I wish I hadn't said.
In anger I have never done a kindly deed or wise,
But many things for which I felt I should apologize.
In looking back across my life, and all I've lost or made,
I can't recall a single time when fury ever paid.
So I struggle to be patient, for I've reached a wiser age;
I do not want to do a thing or speak a word in rage.
I have learned by sad experience that when my temper flies
I never do a worthy thing, a decent deed or wise.

—ANON.

WITH BANNERS

Though I am beaten
   Nobody shall know—
I'll wear defeat so proudly
   I shall go

About my business
   As I did before;
Only, when I have safely
   Closed the door

Against you and the rest,
   Shall I be free
To bow my head—
   When there is none to see

To-night I'll shed my tears;
   To-morrow, when
I talk with you,
   I will be gay again.

Though I am beaten,
   Nobody shall guess;
For I will walk
   As though I knew success.

—ABIGAIL CRESSON

"If only myself could talk to myself
As I knew him a year ago,
I could tell him a lot
That would save him a lot
Of the things he ought to know."

—ANONYMOUS

MY MADONNA

I hailed me a woman from the street,
  Shameless, but, oh, so fair!
I bade her sit in the model's seat
  And I painted her sitting there.

I hid all trace of her heart unclean;
  I painted a babe at her breast;
I painted her as she might have been
  If the Worst had been the Best.

She laughed at my picture and went away.
  Then came, with a knowing nod,
A connoisseur, and I heard him say:
  " 'Tis Mary, the Mother of God."

So I painted a halo round her hair,
  And I sold her and took my fee,
And she hangs in the church of Saint Hillaire,
  Where you and all may see.

—ROBERT SERVICE

LET'S ALL GET TOGETHER

Let's all get together, in ev'rything we do,
No matter if our task is great or small,
Life is quite worth while if we'll only smile.
For the best wins after all,
So when clouds dim our sunshine and dark seems
    the day,
Let's all get together to wear a sunny smile,
And soon the clouds will drift away.

—ANONYMOUS

ADVICE TO THE MARRIED WOMAN

When you marry him, love him.
After you marry him, study him.
If he is honest, honor him.
If he is generous, appreciate him.
When he is sad, cheer him.
When he is talkative, listen to him.
When he is quarrelsome, ignore him.
If he is slothful, spur him.
If he is confidential, encourage him.
If he is noble, praise him.
If he is secretive, trust him.
If he is jealous, cure him.
If he cares naught for pleasure, coax him.
If he favors society, accompany him.
When he deserves it, kiss him.
Let him think how well you understand him; but
    never let him know that you manage him.

—ANON.

PALS

When I see a boy who hasn't a dog
    Or a dog that hasn't a boy,
I think of the lot they are missing
    Of frolic and genuine joy.

Some parents think dogs are a nuisance,
    Just something to bark and annoy;
They can't know how badly a boy needs a dog
    Or how sadly a dog needs a boy.

—MAE NORTON MORRIS

LIFE IS WHAT WE MAKE IT

Let's oftener talk of noble deeds,
    And rarer of the bad ones;
And sing about our happy days,
    And not about the sad ones.
We were not made to fret and sigh,
    And when grief raps to wake it,
Bright happiness is standing by:
    This life is what we make it.

Let's find the sunny side of men
    Or be believers in it;
A light there is in every soul
    That takes the pains to win it.
Oh, there's a slumbering good in all!
    And we perchance may wake it—
Our hands contain the magic wand:
    This life is what we make it.

Then here's to those whose loving hearts
    Shed light and joy about them!
Thanks be to them for countless gems
    We ne'er had known without them.
Oh, this should be a happy world
    To all who may partake it!
The fault's our own if it is not:
    This life is what we make it.

—UNKNOWN

Fashions may come and fashions may go,
    And fads for a short time beguile,
But a person will always look stylish and smart
    When wearing a jovial smile.

—JAMES M. WOODMAN

TRUE VERSES

One day an angel came and asked a king,
    Sated with power, with love of pomp and gold,
Four things that God must dearly love, to bring
    And set them in his presence, so 'tis told.
The king went forth and came again ere night,
    And set before the angel in that hour
A jewelled crown, a scepter gleaming bright,
    A battle weapon, and a throne of power.

The angel's face grew shaded as he gazed
    Upon the king's poor playthings gathered there.
At last his countenance again was raised.
    He said: "These are the trappings pride must wear,
But God's great kingdom knows a richer worth:
    A truer value is its high concern."
"Go," pled the king, "and from the mighty earth
    Bring me these things. I wait for they return."

"Nay, come with me," the angel said, "and I,
    Tho I may lead a long and weary way,
Will show you what is best beneath the sky."
    These are the things he showed the king that day:
A friendly life that served unselfishly,
    A flower that grew in sweetness undefiled,
A fireside where were love and purity,
    The unspoiled spirit of a little child.

              —CLARENCE E. FLYNN

SEASONABLE LIVING

The wisest men you ever knew
    Have never dreamed it treason
To rest a bit—and jest a bit,
    And balance up their reason;
To laugh a bit—and chaff a bit,
    And joke a bit in season.

              —GEORGE WASHINGTON

NOT THIS WAY AGAIN

Whence came and whither bound are we
Holds something still of mystery;
But one grave thought is clear and plain,
We shall not pass this way again.

Why waste an hour in vain regret,
For common ills that must be met?
Why of the thorny road complain?
We shall not pass this way again.

Why wound or cause a tear to start?
Why vex or trouble one poor heart?
Each hath its secret grief or care,
Its burden that thou canst not share.

The years glide by; stand strong and true.
The good thou canst, oh, quickly do!
Let gentle words soothe woe and pain,
We shall not pass this way again.

—ELIZA H. HICOCK

———

Lives of great men, all remind us
　We can make our lives sublime,
And, departing, leave behind us
　Footprints on the sands of time,
Footprints, that perhaps another,
　Sailing o'er life's solemn main,
A forelorn and ship wrecked brother,
　Seeing, shall take heart again.

—HENRY W. LONGFELLOW

A THOUSAND TIMES NO

Intrigue me not with a smile or quip;
I fall no more for a fishing trip. . . .
I've read the folders, but know what is
Implied by "modern conveniences";
So take the children and load the car
With worms and grasshoppers in a jar,
Plus mattresses, and contrive to hoard
A case of beans on the running board.
I'll roast a turkey or bake a ham,
And speed you off with a leg of lamb;
I'll pack the bedding and insect spray,
And wave goodbye as you drive away
To the mountain wilds with your family,
Where everyone has a grand time but me. . . .
What'll I do? Oh, if I must tell,
I'm taking a suite in a swank hotel!

—JANE SAYRE

Beauty originates in your own thought.

How few men are willing to bet on themselves!

Opportunity knocks but once—people are not so considerate.

Beware of the temperamental man who refuses to observe office
hours.

It pays to keep machines in repair—see that you keep your body in
repair, too.

Take time to think—you can do more work with your head than
you can with your feet.

As a man thinks so he does—which explains why some of us do
silly things now and then.

What relief it is to find a man who, when you tell him what you
want done, goes ahead and does it.

DIFFERENCES

The King can drink the best of wine—
    So can I;
And has enough when he would dine—
    So have I;
And cannot order rain or shine—
    Nor can I;
Then where's the difference—let me see—
Betwixt my lord the King and me?

Do trusty friends surround his throne
    Night and day?
Or make his interest their own?
    No, not they.
Mine love me for myself alone—
    Bless'd be they!
And that's the difference which I see
Betwixt my lord the King and me?

Do knaves around me lie in wait
    To deceive?
Or frown and flatter when they hate,
    And would grieve?
Or cruel pomps oppress my state
    By my leave?
No, heaven be thank'd! And here you see
More difference 'twixt the King and me.

He has his fools, with jests and quips
    When he'd play;
He has his armies and his ships—
    Great are they;
But not a child to kiss his lips—
    Well-a-day!
And that's a difference sad to see
Betwixt my lord the King and me.

I wear the cap and he the crown—
    What of that?
I sleep on straw and he on down—
    What of that?
And he's the King and I'm the clown—
    What of that?
If happy I, and wretched he,
Perhaps the King would change with me.

—CHARLES MACKAY

GREETINGS

HOWDY, folks!
Howdy do?
How's the times a-usin' you?
Not so good? Well that's too bad!
Mighty fine? Now ain't I glad!
But perhaps the good ain't so good as it should be,
Perhaps, too, the bad ain't so bad as it could be,
And perhaps we're just av'rage, the whole of us here,
And all pretty good, take it year after year.

Tain't always the good that's the best for a fellow,
Tain't always the bad that's the worst for a fellow!
Hard times may make us,
Riches may break us,
So we'd better keep workin', keep pluggin' ahead,
Us that's downhearted and wishin' we's dead!

—BARTON REES POGUE

THE SKY-LINE TRAIL
(The Muse of a Traveling Man)

I've ridden the trails of the "Sky-Line" way,
From the crest of the great divide,
To the Eastern shores where the dawn of day
Sweeps in with the morning tide—
And I've followed the crest of the "Smokies" west,
Through the land where the setting sun,
Paints a golden streak far beyond each peak,
When the day's long ride is done—
And I'm happy to know that, wherever I go,
In hamlet, or city, or vale,
I can tarry awhile with the friends I know,
All along the "Sky-line Trail."

For the "Sky-line Trail" is more than a way
Over mountain and valley and glen—
'Tis a friendly road that, day by day,
Links the hearts and the souls of men—
And the friends I know on the "Sky-line Trail"
Are men who dwell in the sun,
Who stand four-square in the sunlit air
Of a friendship fairly won;
So whether the road be rough or long,
Or the weather be foul or fair,
I'm sure of a friend to cheer me along,
And a haven of rest somewhere.

Some day, when the sun hangs low in the West,
I shall go for a last long ride,
Through the shadowy trail to that Land of Rest,
Far across the Great Divide—
But I'm sure I'll find at the journey's end
That haven of rest and peace,
Where the Good Book says we shall meet our friends
And abide with the Prince of Peace;
And wherever that be, "I'll be happy I know,
To dwell in that beautiful vale,
With the friends I've known and loved here below,
All along the 'Sky-line Trail'."

—C. A. SNODGRASS

NOTHING LASTS

There is nothing in Life that will always last,
    Son, enjoy Life while yet you may,
For the health that was yours when the morning dawned,
    May, by twilight, be passed away.

And the wealth that you worked for and hardly earned,
    May be yours but a little while,
So the best you can do is to use it so
    That you can, with the whole world, smile.

And some friends that you make may be turned from you
    By a little or trivial thing,
While the others you care for are those who go
    At the parting Life's paths may bring.

You may have both your loves and your passing hates,
    But when love, just as hate is passed,
Then you realize keenly again the fact
    There is nothing in Life will last.

And to many 'tis strange and to many queer,
    This, for all, is the way things go,
But the fact there is nothing in Life that lasts
    Is the truth we must finally know.

            —FRANCIS JAMES YOUNGBLOOD

Gather ye rose-buds while ye may,
    Old Time is still a flying
And this same flower that smiles today,
    To-morrow will be dying.

            —HERRICK

THE STRANGER

If there comes to you a stranger
Who is weary, who is hungry,
Sore beset by Evil Spirits,
Seeking for a place to rest in**
Seeking for a place of shelter;
Give him of your food and garments,
Give him of your love and friendship,
Make a place within your wigwam
Where he, too, may find contentment:
Send him on his journey, happy;
Send him forth, with strength and gladness
In his mind and in his body:
That your life may be remembered
By the Father of Creation,
And your waking hours more pleasant,
And your sleeping be more restful**
That your days shall be the longer
In the Land of the Ojibway.

—HOTAN-TONKA

CROSSING THE BAR

Sunset and evening Star, and one clear call for me,
And may there be no moaning of the bar, when I put out to sea.
But such a tide as moving seems asleep, too full for sound and foam,
When that which drew from out the boundless deep, turns again home.
Twilight and evening bell and after that the dark!
And may there be no sadness or farewell, when I embark;
For tho' from out the bourne of time and place The flood may bear me far,
I hope to see my Pilot face to face, when I have crossed the bar.

—ALFRED TENNYSON

YOU SAID

You said:
Always and always I shall remember
This one perfect day.
Life may go on from now,
Yet this was happiness too complete
To leave even the shadow of a shadow of regret.

No October sun shall ever shine again
Upon your tawny head that's half so warm as this.
No vine-leaves fleck with such pure silver the white
Still radiance of your arms.
No sunlight deep in any mountain brook
Catch so warm a glint of summer in your eyes.

And though I grow old, you said,
I shall remember always.

And I, to whom the day had been
Just one more happy day,
Laughed when you spoke.

But now I sit alone, remembering.

—ANONYMOUS

_____

"I walked a mile with Pleasure,
   She chattered all the way,
But she left me none the wiser
   For all she had to say.

"I walked a mile with Sorrow,
   And ne'er a word said she;
But, oh, the things I learned from her
   When Sorrow walked with me."

—ANONYMOUS

THE CABIN ON THE HOMESTEAD

There's a cabin on the homestead
   In a valley far away;
Where the pines are always sighing,
   And the lazy breezes play.

There's a creek that's ever winding,
   Ever winding to the sea;
Just a silver ribbon gleaming
   In a land that's far and free.

There's a mother ever waiting
   And a light that ever shines
In the cabin on the homestead;
   And a tie that ever binds.

But they've roped me in the city
   And I guess I'm doomed to stay,
While ever my mind's a-wand'ring,
   And ever my mem'ries stray.

Dreaming, dreaming, ever dreaming
   While my eyes grow dim with age;
Drifting, drifting, ever drifting,
   Life is passing page by page.

E'er I long for the solitudes
   Stretched beneath the Milky Way;
To dream alone, the world my own
   In the evening's dusky gray.

To sit at night, in dreamy light
   Of my campfire's flapping flare;
To rest in peace, where worries cease,
   Forgotten, the world of care.

Oh, I'd love to ditch my collars
    And my jewel-studded shirt;
Leave behind the smoke-screened cities
    And their sorrow, noise and dirt.

Just to sit again and ponder
    On the banks of that old stream;
Not a care, a task, a sorrow,
    Just to sit and dream and dream.

But life drives us ever onward,
    One step backward and we fail;
And grim duties ever lead us
    O'er a rough and winding trail.

So I must forget my dreaming
    Of the days that used to be,
And the cabin on the homestead;
    For no more will I be free.

                    —ROY THOMAS GREENUP

FULLY DRESSED!

It never matters much to me
    What kind of hat or gown you wear,
I'm always looking at your face
    To see if any smile is there.

And when I see you looking glad
    And smiling just a bit,
I seem to note, Unconsciously,
    How well your hat and costume fit!

                    —CAROLYN HOLMES SMITH

THE GOOD SAMARITAN

A stranger trod the road to Jericho,
    That rugged winding road, where oft the thief
    Waylays and brings good citizens to grief.
The robbers beat, then stripped and laid him low,
Bereft, beset, and marked by cruel blow.
    A Priest went by, but offered no relief,
    A Levite, too, then came, and past belief,
They left him there and on their way did go.

The Good Samaritan approached, and there
    Beside the stricken man, in cruel need,
    He demonstrated well the service creed.
He dressed those open wounds, an action rare,
And bound the grievous hurts with extreme care.
    To render full the measure of his deed,
    Unto the wayside inn he turned with speed,
And to the landlord paid the stranger's fare.

Are you the Priest, or yet the Levite, who
    Doth pass upon the rugged winding road,
    But offers not to share the stranger's load?
Do you pass by the man in trouble, too,
And turn your back, as many folks oft do?
    Are you the Good Samaritan, whose code
    Restores the man in highway or abode,
To bring him back with strength and courage new?

—HARRY BROKAW

"Give to your enemy forgiveness.
Give to your opponent tolerance.
Give to your friends your heart.
Give to your child a good example.
Give to your parents deference.
Give to everybody sunshine."

—ANONYMOUS

SOMETIMES

Sometimes I long for a lazy isle,
Ten thousand miles from home,
Where the warm sun shines and the blue sky smiles
And the milk-white breakers foam—
A coral island, bravely set
In the midst of the southern sea
Away from the hurry and noise and fret
Forever surrounding me!

For I tire of labor and care and fight,
And I weary of plan and scheme,
And ever and ever my thoughts take flight
To the island of my dream.
And I fancy drowsing the whole day long
In a hammock that gently swings—
Away from the clamorous toiling throng,
Away from the swirl of things!

And yet I know in a little while,
When the first glad hours were spent,
I'd sicken and tire of my lazy isle
And cease to be content!
I'd hear the call of the world's great game—
The battle with gold and men—
And I'd sail once more, with heart of flame,
Back to the game again!

—BERTON BRALEY

THE SPELL OF THE YUKON

I wanted the gold, and I sought it;
  I scrabbled and mucked like a slave.
Was it famine or scurvy—I fought it;
  I hurled my youth into a grave.
I wanted the gold, and I got it—
  Came out with a fortune last fall—
Yet somehow life's not what I thought it,
  And somehow the gold isn't all.

No! There's the land. (Have you seen it?)
  It's the loneliest land that I know,
From the big, dizzy mountains that screen it
  To the deep, deathlike valleys below.
Some say God was tired when He made it;
  Some say it's a fine land to shun;
Maybe; but there's some as would trade it
  For no land on earth—and I'm one.

You come to get rich (very good reason);
  You feel like an exile at first;
You hate it like hell for a season,
  And then you are worse than the worst.
It grips you like some kinds of sinning;
  It twists you from foe to a friend;
It seems it's been since the beginning;
  It seems it will be to the end.

I've stood in some mighty-mouthed hollow
  That's plumb-full of hush to the brim;
I've watched the big, husky sun wallow
  In crimson and gold, and grow dim,

Till the moon set the pearly peaks gleaming,
  And the stars tumbled out, neck and crop;
And I've thought that I surely was dreaming,
  With the peace o' the world piled on top.

The summer—no sweeter was ever;
  The sunshiny woods all athrill;
The gravling aleap in the river,
  The bighorn asleep on the hill.
The strong life that never knows harness;
  The wilds where the caribou call;
The freshness, the freedom, the farness—
  O God! how I'm stuck on it all.

The winter! the brightness that blinds you,
  The white land locked tight as a drum,
The cold fear that follows and finds you,
  The silence that bludgeons you dumb.
The snows that are older than history,
  The woods where the weird shadows slant;
The stillness, the moonlight, the mystery,
  I've bade 'em good-by—but I can't.

There's a land where the mountains are nameless,
  And the rivers all run God knows where;
There are lives that are erring and aimless,
  And deaths that just hang by a hair;
There are hardships that nobody reckons;
  There are valleys unpeopled and still;
There's a land—oh, it beckons and beckons,
  And I want to go back—and I will.

They're making my money diminish;
   I'm sick of the taste of champagne.
Thank God! when I'm skinned to a finish
   I'll pike to the Yukon again.
I'll fight—and you bet it's no sham-fight;
   It's hell!—but I've been there before;
And it's better than this by a long-sight—
   So me for the Yukon once more.

There's gold, and it's haunting and haunting;
   It's luring me on as of old;
Yet it isn't the gold that I'm wanting
   So much as just finding the gold.
It's the great, big, broad land 'way up yonder,
   It's the forests where silence has lease;
It's the beauty that thrills me with wonder,
   It's the stillness that fills me with peace.

—ROBERT SERVICE

KINDNESS

I often wonder why people do not make more of the marvelous power there is in Kindness. It is the greatest lever to move the hearts of men that the world has ever known—greater by far than anything that mere ingenuity can devise or subtlety suggest. Kindness is the kingpin of success in life; it is the prime factor in overcoming friction and making the human machinery run smoothly. If a man is your enemy you cannot disarm him in any other way so surely as by doing him a kind act. The meanest brute that ever drew breath is not altogether insensible to the influence of kindness. . . . .

Kindness makes the whole world akin. It breaks down the barriers of distrust, deceit, envy, jealousy, hate and all their miserable train.

—ANDREW CHAPMAN

I HATE TO BE A KICKER

I hate to be a kicker,
    I always long for peace,
But the wheel that does the squeaking
    Is the one that gets the grease.

You tell 'em, Kid—you're peaceful
    And not too hard to please,
But the dog that's always scratching
    Is the one that has the fleas.

"I hate to be a kicker"
    Means nothing in a show;
The kicker in the chorus
    Is the one that gets the dough.

The art of soft soap spreading
    Is a thing that palls and stales,
But the guy who wields the hammer
    Is the one who drives the nails.

Let us not put any notions
    That are harmful in your head,
But the baby that keeps yelling
    Is the baby that gets fed.

—ST. PAUL OPTIMIST NEWS

"I SAW GOD WASH THE WORLD LAST NIGHT"

"I saw God wash the world last night
With His sweet showers on high;
And then when morning came
I saw Him hang it out to dry.

He washed each tiny blade of grass,
And every trembling tree;
He flung His showers against the hills
And swept the billowing sea.

The white rose is a cleaner white,
The red rose is more red,
Since God washed every fragrant face
And put them all to bed.

There's not a bird, there's not a bee
That wings along the way,
But is a cleaner bird and bee
Than it was yesterday.

I saw God wash the world last night;
Ah, would he had washed me
As clean of all my dust and dirt
As that old white birch tree!"

—DR. WILLIAM L. STIDGER

THE STAY-AT-HOME

You may sing your songs to the frozen North,
    To the land of the hidden gold,
Where the snow-capped mountains mutely bid
    A challenge to those who are bold.

You may sing your songs to the torrid South,
    Where fevers will madden the brain,
Where only the men of the staunchest stuff
    Are fit to return home again.

You may sing your songs to the desert waste,
    To treks o'er the blistering sands;
You may sing your songs to hunger and thirst
    In the depths of far-away lands.

But don't forget when you're speaking about
    The countries where virile men roam
To mention, in passing, a word of praise
    To the brave souls who stay at home.

There's courage required of those who defy
    The dangers and hardships unseen,
But there's courage, too, in the heart of those
    Who stick to the daily routine.

For it takes a heart that is stout and strong
    To stand the monotonous ways
Of a Life that is fraught with drab events
    In a City of Changeless Days.

—ROBERT W. KERNAGHAN

LAZARUS

I shall not ever trouble you again.
I came to you for comfort on a night
When I had known the weight of woe, and fright,
When I was beaten with the whips of pain.

I came to you for comfort of a kiss
Pressed gently on my tear-wet, tired eyes,
For arms about my shoulders, weary wise—
Since I have need of you at times like this.

I came to you for just the meagre crumbs
From your full table; but I was denied.
And I could salvage nothing from my pride,
For I had come as any beggar comes.

You had a guest! And what was there to say?
I know my scarlet rags were out of place,
And I am glad the shadows hid my face.
My need is not so great as yesterday.

For I have gnawed the roots of old desire,
And bruised my lips against a cup of gall.
Outside, but in the crannies of your wall
I burned my hands against a dying fire.

Tomorrow's moon may rise and slowly wane,
And you may spread your fare with lavish hand,
But I am wiser now. . . I understand,
And I shall never trouble you again!

—CARMEN JUDSON

BACK TO THE FARM

"I'll buy a little farm somewhere," the old man says, "and tinker there until it's time to go to sleep, down where the bending willows weep. I know a farm I'd like to buy; it's where I lived when three feet high. It's where my father used to strive to keep the family alive. 'Twas there, in bygone, golden days, I hoed the beans and husked the maize, and dreamed of triumphs I'd achieve, when I that dreary farm could leave. To dwell in cities was my aim, to cut a swath and conquer fame, and that old sandy, rocky farm for me was quite devoid of charm. The dreams I dreamed have all come true, I've done the things I meant to do, but I am old and worn and tired, and for a long time I've desired, above all other things, to go back to the scenes I used to know." Thousands of old men talk that way; when they are bent by the years, and gray, feeble of step and weak of arms, they turn their eyes to the old home farm.

—WALT MASON

Be strong! We are not here to play, to dream, to drift;
We have hard work to do and loads to lift;
Shun not the struggle: face it—'tis God's gift.
    Be strong, be strong!

Be strong! Say not the days are evil—Who's to blame?
And fold the hands and acquiesce—O shame!
Stand up, speak out, and bravely, in God's name,
    Be strong, be strong!

Be strong! It matters not how deep entrenched the wrong,
How hard the battle goes, the day, how long;
Faint not, fight on! Tomorrow comes the song,
    Be strong, be strong!

—MATTIE D. BABCOCK

AS YOU GO THROUGH LIFE

Don't look for flaws as you go through life,
  And even when you find them,
It is wise and kind to be somewhat blind
  And look for the virtue behind them.

For the cloudiest night has a hint of light
  Somewhere in its shadows hiding;
It's better by far to hunt for a star
  Than the spots on the sun abiding.

The current of life runs ever away
  To the bosom of God's great ocean—
Don't set your force 'gainst the river's course,
  And think to alter its motion.

Don't waste a curse on the universe,
  Remember, it lived before you;
Don't butt at the storm with your puny form,
  But bend and let it go o'er you.

The world will never adjust itself
  To suit your whims to the letter;
Some things must go wrong your whole life long,
  And the sooner you know it the better.

It is folly to fight with the infinite,
  And go under at last in the wrestle;
The wiser man shapes into God's plan
  As water shapes into a vessel.

—ELLA WHEELER WILCOX

DOCTOR BILL

Did you ever know a doctor
   Whom the kids were glad to see?
I know just such a doctor,
   And he lives not far from me.
Most kids are scared of doctors,
   But my kids when they're ill
Are just as happy as can be,
   When I call Doctor Bill.

He's a different sort of doctor—
   He treats kiddies with a smile,
While he patches up their scratches
   He keeps clowning all the while.
And they never will refuse him,
   When he says, "Here, take this pill."
But take it down without a frown
   To please Ole Doctor Bill.

The kids just all adore him,
   They're happy as can be
To have him call, he's not at all
   A man of dignity,
Who scares the kids with great big words,
   And looks that fairly kill.
He makes them laugh and they're not half
   As sick with Doctor Bill.

—E. CLAYTON HAZELWOOD

AM I ASKING TOO MUCH?

Am I asking too much
    When I ask for a chance
To share in all things
    That living demands?

Am I asking too much
    When I ask to be tried,
When I'm willing to work
    If work be supplied?

Am I asking too much
    When I ask for a nook
With flowers and trees
    By some whispering brook?

Am I asking too much
    When I ask for a chance
To build me a nest
    And have any romance?

And that will I ask
    And that will I plead,
The same for my brother,
    Whatever his creed.

Am I asking too much?
Am I asking too much?

—ABEL SCHNADER

IF I SHOULD DIE TONIGHT

If I should die tonight,
My friends would look upon my quiet face
Before they laid it in its resting place,
And deem that death had left it almost fair;
And, laying snow-white flowers against my hair,
Would fold it down with tearful tenderness,
And fold my hands with lingering caress—
Poor hands, so empty and so cold tonight!

If I should die tonight,
My friends would call to mind, with loving thought,
Some loving deed the icy hands had wrought;
Some gentle word the frozen lips had said;
Errands on which the willing feet had sped;
The memory of my selfishness and pride,
My hasty words, would all be put aside,
And so I should be loved and mourned tonight.

If I should die tonight,
Even hearts estranged should turn once more to me,
Recalling other days remorsefully;
The eyes that chill me with averted glance
Would look upon me as of yore, perchance,
And soften, in the old familiar way;
For who could war with dumb unconscious clay!
So I might rest, forgiven of all, tonight.

Oh, friends, I pray tonight,
Keep not your kisses for my dead cold brow—
The way is lonely, let me feel them now.
Think gently of me; I am travel-worn;
My faltering feet are pierced with many a thorn.
Forgive, oh, hearts estranged, forgive, I plead!
When dreamless rest is mine I shall not need
The tenderness for which I long tonight.

—ARABELLA E. SMITH

THAT SILVER HAIRED DADDY OF MINE

In a vine covered shack in the mountains
  Bravely fighting the battle of time,
There's a dear one whose weathered life's sorrows
  He's that silver haired daddy of mine.

CHORUS

If I could recall all the heartaches,
  Dear old daddy I've caused you to bear,
If I could erase those lines from your face
And bring back the gold to your hair,
And if God would but grant me the power
  Just to turn back the pages of time,
I'd give all I own if I could atone
  To that silver haired daddy of mine.

Oh, I know it's too late, dear old daddy,
  To recall all those sorrows and cares,
For dear mother is waiting in Heaven
  Just to comfort and solace you there.

(Sold for the benefit of the Blind)

THE CAMP FIRE

"Did you ever watch the camp fire
  When the wood had fallen low;
And the ashes start to whiten
  Round the embers' crimson glow;
With the night sounds all around you
  Making silence doubly sweet;
And a full moon high above you
  That the spell may be complete?
Tell me, were you ever nearer
  To the land of heart's desire,
Than when you sat there thinking
  With your face turned toward the fire?"

—R. L. STEVENSON

WE HAVE LIVED AND LOVED TOGETHER

We have lived and loved together
   Through many changing years;
We have shared each other's gladness
   And wept each other's tears;
I have known ne'er a sorrow
   That was long unsoothed by thee;
For thy smiles can make a summer
   Where darkness else would be.

Like the leaves that fall around us
   In autumn's fading hours,
Are the traitor's smiles, that darken
   When the cloud of sorrow lowers;
And though many such we've known, love,
   Too prone, alas, to range,
We both can speak of one love
   Which time can never change.

We have lived and loved together
   Through many changing years,
We have shared each other's gladness
   And wept each other's tears.
And let us hope the future,
   As the past has been will be:
I will share with thee my sorrows,
   And thou thy joys with me.

—UNKNOWN

ON MY LAST DAY

Let it be Spring
On my last day!

A Spring of tender green . . . of sunshine . . .
Filled with promises of life . . .
Not death.   And let the lilacs
Spill their purple bloom beside the wall,
So that I may forget
How dead leaves fall.

Let nature lend her gayest mood
To speed me on my way.
So many tears I've known . . .
Let me remember naught but smiles
On my last day.

May there be young birds whispering
Above me in the trees,
A sudden rush of warm sweet rain
On thirsty leaves,
A rainbow and a cricket's chirp,
An awkward lamb at play. . . .

Oh, God of living things . . .
Let it be Spring
On my last day!

—FRANCESCA FALK MILLER

THE FRIENDLY MAN

There's a man comes down our street; he brings my mamma's mail,
An' every day I watch for him from inside our front rail.
'Coz he don't say, "Aw, ain't he cute!" nor call me pretty names,
An' he don't tell me to be good, an' say, "Be careful, James."
I'd love my ma a whole lot more if she'd just talk like him,
An' holler out, "Hello, old scout!" or else, "Good mornin', Jim!"

—ANONYMOUS

JUST LEARNING

We used to live in a grand old place,
White pillared doors, and vines to trace
The millionaire's crest on the marbled walls**
A chauffeur and maids and butler for calls.
Oh, you know the type, the regular thing,
Grounds and the palace, made for a king.
But to tell the truth we were lonely there.
Folks seemed to think us something rare

Just 'cause we lived in so splendid a place.
Then hard times slapped us full in the face.
And, oh, how it stung, and how deeply it cut,
To part with the past and those lovely things—but
In losing we found through the sharp wrench of pain
A whole heap of friends, a far greater gain.
The little old lady down the street
Thumping home from work on unsteady feet;

The boy next door and his mongrel pup;
The little lame girl six houses up;
The grocery boy and the iceman, too;
The beggar who comes to ask for a sou
And who strangely seems to understand
When you show him only an empty hand;
Who turns away with a cheerful smile
And a heart-wringing word: "Better for all in a little
    while."

Yes, the sun shines brighter than ever before.
The darkest clouds can't darken our sunny door,
And the rain on the roof—well, yes, it does leak,
But, oh, the music the raindrops speak!
And somehow the deeper you seem to get hurt
The greater your wisdom, your soul's more alert,
The keener all joys, the brighter the light,
The clearer the promise of Day after Night.

—DOROTHY B. HOLMBERG

THESE ARE THE DAYS

Those were the happy days.
　　We did not know it then.
Each hour we travel ways
　　We shall not walk again.
But then it is the thorn
　　We note, and not the rose,
Nor think about the morn
　　Until the evening's close.

Those were the happy years.
　　But then we did not guess
Each hour a path appears
　　Of simple happiness.
But then we think, alas,
　　Our joys are not so great,
And never know they pass
　　Until it is too late.

These are the happy times.
　　We do not know it, yet.
But like remembered rimes
　　We never shall forget,
These are the days, somehow,
　　That older years shall praise.
I wish we knew it now—
　　These are the happy days.

　　　　　　　　　—DOUGLAS MALLOCH

―――――

There is no remedy for time misspent;
　　No healing for the waste of idleness,
Whose very languor is a punishment
　　Heavier than active souls can feel or guess.

　　　　　　　　　—SIR A. DE VERE

LULLABY

They brought that bit of her in haste away:
That little hope that somehow had to die,
And all night long I heard the girl-bride sing
A lullaby—

A lullaby she oftentimes had sung,
As smiling she sat stitching tiny seams
On delicate, exquisite little things,
Dreaming her dreams.

And now . . . the dull gray ward echoes the tune
As hours drag by while fever sways her brain.
"Rock-a-by my baby—Rock-a-by"
Comes the refrain.

At dawn they pulled the sheet above her face.
Her man stood by the bed, his hands clenched tight.
The nurse in silence drew the dull green shade
And snuffed the light.

The tall, gaunt poplars nodded in the breeze.
Their melancholic rustling seemed a sigh
Waking in lulling cadence once again—
The lullaby.

—ROSA ZAGNONI MARINONI

THE ANGELS WILL NOT SING

The angels will not sing this year;
They told the Lord we did not care,
And the Lord said that it was fair
That, since it seemed we did not care,
   The angels need not sing:

      And on earth peace
      To men, goodwill
      And peace on earth,
      Goodwill to men.

"They have no peace," the angels said,
"Goodwill is gone and hope is dead—
They do not care," the angels said
"That peace, goodwill, and hope are dead,
   There is no need to sing:"

      And on earth peace
      To men, goodwill
      And peace on earth,
      Goodwill to men.

The age-old song will not be heard;
The angels will not bring the work.
The Lord has said (He will be heard)
That, since we still refuse the Word,
   The angels need not sing:

      And on earth peace
      To men, goodwill
      And peace on earth,
      Goodwill to men.

We did not hear the silence there—
We did not hear—we did not care—
But oh, there was a silence there,
   There was no song—we did not care.

                 —GENEVIEVE PAUL

THE HOUSE BY THE SIDE OF
THE ROAD

There are hermit souls that live withdrawn
In the peace of their self-content;
There are souls, like stars, that dwell apart,
In a fellowless firmament;
There are pioneer souls that blaze their paths
Where highways never ran—
But let me live by the side of the road
And be a friend to man.

Let me live in a house by the side of the road,
Where the race of men go by—
The men who are good and the men who are bad,
As good and as bad as I.
I would not sit in the scorner's seat,
Or hurl the cynic's ban—
Let me live in a house by the side of the road
And be a friend to man.

I see from my house by the side of the road,
By the side of the highway of life,
The men who press with the ardor of hope,
The men who are faint with the strife.
But I turn not away from their smiles nor their tears—
Both, parts of an infinite plan—
Let me live in my house by the side of the road
And be a friend to man.

I know there are brook-gladdened meadows ahead
And mountains of wearisome height;
That the road passes on through the long afternoon
And stretches away to the night.
But still I rejoice when the travelers rejoice,
And weep with the strangers that moan,
Nor live in my house by the side of the road
Like a man who dwells alone.

Let me live in my house by the side of the road
Where the race of men go by—
They are good, they are bad, they are weak, they are strong,
Wise, foolish—so am I.
Then why should I sit in the scorner's seat
Or hurl the cynic's ban?—
Let me live in my house by the side of the road
And be a friend to man.

—SAM WALTER FOSS

MY HEART

Let my heart be a gate
So strong and stout,
That envy, lust, and hate
Are shut without;
And let it be a door
Foes cannot spin,
That love, forevermore,
Bide safe within.

—LALIA MITCHELL THORNTON

IN MEMORIAM

LOUIS HENRY CLEMENT
OBIIT MAY 29TH, 1926, SALISBURY, N. C.

What a gentle spirit passed into the Great Beyond when Louis Henry Clement died!

I stood today, with loving friends, beside his bier, in that old home where he had lived for two score years and ten.

From out God's Holy Writ the preacher read: "Let not your heart be troubled."

I wiped away my tears and looked toward the West, where golden sunbeams wrought strange figures on the sky.

I saw him beckon me; I heard him call: "Hail and farewell!"

I shall not see his like again.

His heart knew not what malice was;

His lips could speak no guile;

His hands could work no cunning.

Forgive me, Lord! I mean not to be impious when I say: "Thou couldst not, out of dust, create a nobler man."

He was my friend; I loved him.

O gentle Christ, receive his soul!

—CHARLES W. TILLETT

CHARLOTTE, MAY 30TH, 1926

YOU HELPED THE DUMB

Just in a dream I stood at Heaven's gate,
St. Peter met me with his Book of Fate—
A pond'rous volume bound in glist'ning gold,
With letters large that stood out clear and bold;
He thought awhile, then shook his hoary head—
"The records show but few good deeds," he said.
"And not enough to merit Heaven, I fear;
To me your prospects, friend, look rather drear."
He traced the scanty items with his thumb,
When, lo! he stopped and said, "You helped the dumb—
You took a stray cat in, two dogs you fed,
And to the birds you gave some crusts of bread.
Ah, yes! you did your best to aid the weak,
God's little folk, the ones that could not speak;
So enter thou, and join the angel-band,
There is a place for you at God's right hand."

—WILLA HOEY

THE FURROW

Plowman, plow your furrow straight
    Make your furrow clean and long,
Hold your plow with master grip,
    Let your work be firm and strong.

Plowman, smell the new turned loam,
    Dust like that which gave us birth.
Let your lusty strength increase
    With each time you touch the earth.

Are not stories told by men
    Of a plowman and his star?
Plowman, plow your furrow long—
    Round the world is not too far!

—J. E. ELLIOTT

IN THE MARKET PLACE

I saw you in the market place today,
Tall—so tall!—and bronzed and uniformed,
And my heart shook in me—failed—
My throat closed on the swift pain that filled it.
You stood beside me, your eyes on mine in the old fashion,
And all the years between were gone like a wind on the mountains.
Gone was the doubt—if doubt has been—
And back on your heart I lay in spirit
Hushed to the tune of tears.
Oh, gem within the casket of heart!
Oh, secret light in my lone shadow depths!
Oh, perfect pearl of joy drowned in the wine of everlasting loss!
This anguished ecstacy of souls' embrace,
This speechless moment in the market place!

—VINGIE E. ROE

I WENT TO TOWN

I went to town last night and rode
    A street so brightly lit,
That glaring lights soon dazzled me,
    And I got lost in it.

To-day I found a still green wood,
    Seldom traversed by men,
Alone I walked and dreamed awhile,
    And found myself again.

—EMMA KEILER

VISION IN SOLITUDE

I looked into the very heart of life,
And witnessed all eternity at once;
Saw men who build our bridges, lay our streets,
Dig our sewers and rear our cities high;
Saw men of medicine whose lonely work
Bears fruit of comfort easing pain and fear,
Whose fingers smooth the paths of consciousness
From birth to death, and I saw, also, men
Who frame financial systems, men whose strength
Upholds the world of men.   All these I saw;
Then saw a poet scratching pretty words
On snowy paper for an audience
Of mild old women.   But his progeny
Shall lift to greater worth; their thought shall save
This artificial world from hunger void,
When demon progress turns against itself.

—GAYLORD PARKS

UNANSWERED PRAYER

He asked for strength that he might achieve; he was made weak
that he might obey.

He asked for health that he might do greater things; he was given
infirmity that he might do better things.

He asked for riches that he might be happy; he was given poverty
that he might be wise.

He asked for power that he might have the praise of men; he was
given weakness that he might feel the need of God.

He asked for all things that he might enjoy life; he was given Life
that he might enjoy all things.

—UNKNOWN

THE LONELY LILY

Midst the flowers in the garden,
  Midst the roses scarlet red,
Grew a lonely, gentle lily
  With her tender, snow-white head.

And I asked this lonely lily
  How it was that one so fair
Lived 'midst bold and gaudy flowers,
  With such ostentatious air.

And she looked at me so gaily—
  Soft her answer I could hear,
In hear peaceful lily language,
  Sweet and mellow to the ear:

"Speak no ill to me of roses,
  With their petals scarlet bright;
Were my fellows only lilies,
  I should not be in your sight."

—ABEL SCHNADER

A WOMAN'S PHILOSOPHY OF LIFE

To guard my doors—yet welcome all who come;
  Stick to my job—not poach on other people's;
Forget myself and soul—be priest of home,
  Since roads to heaven climb stairs as well as steeples;
To live my life, and leave my children theirs,
  Exacting nought that is not freely given;
To laugh at life—not think that preference shares
  In gloom on earth can earn me joy in heaven.

—JOCELYN C. LEA

AN UNFINISHED SONG

One day in the glad Springtime, my love,
    When all the world way gay,
You whispered low, "Let us sing a song
    As we journey along life's way!"
And with one accord our voices rose
    In a fine harmonious strain,
Till the distant woods sent back the notes
    Of the tender, soft refrain.

But you grew tired of the song, my love,
    Ere the theme was half complete,
And your rich voice ceased, while the last faint strains
    Floated off into cadence sweet.
Then bravely I struggled to sing my part,
    But the notes died away in a groan,
And I burst into tears, for I hadn't the heart
    To finish the song alone.

—DAISIE L. SMALING

LET ME CALL YOU SWEETHEART

Let me call you sweet-heart,
I'm in love with you.
Let me hear you whisper
That you love me too.
Keep the love-light glowing
In your eyes so true—
Let me call you sweet-heart,
I'm in love with you.

—COPYRIGHT, HAROLD ROSSITER

LOST DAYS

The lost days of my life until to-day,
What were they, could I see them on the street
Lie as they fell? Would they be ears of wheat
Sown once for food but trodden into clay?
Or golden coins squandered and still to pay?
Or drops of blood dabbling the guilty feet?
Or such spilt water as in dreams must cheat
The undying throats of Hell, athirst always?

I do not see them here; but after death
God knows I know the faces I shall see,
Each one a murdered self, with low last breath.
"I am thyself—what hast thou done to me?"
"And I—and I—thyself," (lo! each one saith),
"And thou thyself to all eternity!"

—DANTE GABRIEL ROSSETTI

MAIN STREET

Little towns are friendly towns,
    I'll take Main Street any day,
And the fun of greeting neighbors
    As I walk its narrow way.

Your pockets can be empty,
    But you're richer than a king,
Just walk a block on Main Street,
    Greet the friends all small towns bring.

—RAYMOND C. CAUEFFIELD

THE PARSON'S SON

This is the song of the parson's son, as he squats in his shack
alone,

On the wild, weird nights, when the Northern Lights shoot up
from the frozen zone,

And it's sixty below, and couched in the snow the hungry
huskies moan:

"I'm one of the Arctic brotherhood, I'm an old-time pioneer.

I came with the first—O God! how I've cursed this Yukon—
but still I'm here.

I've sweated athirst in its summer heat, I've frozen and starved
in its cold;

I've followed my dreams by its thousand streams, I've toiled and
moiled for its gold.

"Look at my eyes—been snow-blind twice; look where my foot's
half gone;

And that gruesome scar on my left cheek, where the frost-fiend
bit to the bone.

Each one a brand of this devil's land, where I've played and I've
lost the game,

A broken wreck with a craze for 'Hooch,' and never a cent to
my name.

"This mining is only a gamble; the worst is as good as the best;

I was in with the bunch and I might have come out right on top
with the rest;

With Cormack, Ladue and Macdonald—O God! but it's hell to
think

Of the thousands and thousands I've squandered on cards and
women and drink.

"In the early days we were just a few, and we hunted and fished
    around,
Nor dreamt by our lonely camp-fire of the wealth that lay under
    the ground.
We traded in skins and whiskey, and I've often slept under the
    shade
Of that lone birch tree on Bonanza, where the first big find
    was made.

"We were just like a great big family, and every man had his
    squaw,
And we lived such a wild, free, fearless life beyond the pale of
    the law;
Till sudden there came a whisper, and it maddened us every man,
And I got in on Bonanza before the big rush began.

"Oh, those Dawson days, and the sin and the blaze, and the
    town all open wide!
(If God made me in His likeness, sure He let the devil inside.)
But we all were mad, both the good and the bad, and as for
    the women, well—
No spot on the map in so short a space had hustled more souls
    to hell.

"Money was just like dirt there, easy to get and to spend.
I was all caked in on a dance-hall jade, but she shook me in the end.
It put me queer, and for near a year I never drew sober breath,
Till I found myself in the bughouse ward with a claim staked
    out on death.

"Twenty years in the Yukon, struggling along its creeks;
Roaming its giant valleys, scaling its God-like peaks;
Bathed in its fiery sunsets, fighting its fiendish cold—
Twenty years in the Yukon . . . twenty years—and I'm old.

"Old and weak, but no matter, there's 'hooch' in the bottle still.

I'll hitch up the dogs to-morrow, and mush down the trail to Bill.

It's so long dark, and I'm lonesome—I'll just lay down on the bed;

To-morrow I'll go . . . to-morrow . . . I guess I'll play on the red.

". . . Come, Kit, your pony is saddled. I'm waiting, dear, in the court . . .

. . . Minnie, you devil, I'll kill you if you skip with that flossy sport . . .

. . . How much does it go to the pan, Bill? . . .

. . . Our Father, which are in heaven, hallowed be Thy name . . ."

This was the song of the parson's son, as he lay in his bunk alone,

Ere the fire went out and the cold crept in, and his blue lips ceased to moan,

And the hunger-maddened malamutes had torn his flesh from bone.

—ROBERT SERVICE

EXPIRED

"Boys, I've quit the hold-up game
I'll hang around joints no more."
So with a sigh
And a faint little cry
The garter stretched out on the floor.

—JAZZ

"INASMUCH"

I led a blind man 'cross a busy street on yestermorn. His humble dress, his lowly mien, marked him as one rejected and despised of men.

He walked so feebly, I did fear that he would fall beneath the cruel juggernauts of trade. He spoke no word of thanks at parting, only this in a faltering voice: "God will Himself reward you, sir!"

A Boy Scout saw me do it. He waved at me and ran with all his speed to lift a crippled Negro granny up from where she helpless lay.

A lordly officer, unused to deeds of kindness, beholding what I did, raised high his bludgeon in the air and stayed the traffic's onrush. Then, he took from out a frightened mother's arms a little babe and bore it to the other side with tenderest care.

A haughty dame, caparison'd in costly furs, heard what the blind man said to me. Her scornful face became suffused with light of love as she stooped low and placed within a beggar's outstretched hand a goodly sum.

An elm tree in a park hardby peered at me with its glistening eyes and clapped its frostbit hands approvingly. A violet, half hid beneath a fallen leaf, looked up at me with blue eyed smile as though it fain would let me know that my small deed like its small life made happiness abound.

And when I came to where I do my customary stint, all those with whom I labor by day bestowed on me unwonted acts of tenderness and love. A wealthy client came whose heart I thought was flint. He brought the Will and Testament that I had writ for him and said: "I pray you add a codicil and give unto the orphaned poor one-half of all that I possess."

Another came and said: "I beg that you withdraw from off the records of the court the suit I brought against my former friend wherein I charged him with a grievous wrong."

And when the evening shadows came, a holy peace that I had never known before possessed my soul. I laid me down and slept with sweet content; and as the old hall-clock tolled out twelve strokes, announcing that another day was done, I felt a kindly touch that waked me. Behold! The blind man stood beside my bed!

A light, mysterious, made my narrow chamber bright as noonday sun, and there before my wondering eyes a heavenly metamorphosis took place. The blind man's sightless balls glowed with a fire divine, his humble garb was changed into a royal vestment—his countenance was like the countenance of an angel. He spread his hands in benediction over me; nail prints were there! His garments parted and I saw a spear thrust in his side!

The Vision, vanishing, thrilled my unworthy heart with words no mortal tongue dare utter; "INASMUCH AS THOU DIDST IT UNTO ONE OF THE LEAST OF THESE MY BRETHREN, THOU DIDST IT UNTO ME!"

Lo! The blind man that I led across the street on yestermorn was CHRIST, MY LORD AND KING!

—Selected

BE CONSIDERATE

When you get to know a fellow, know his joys
and know his cares,

When you come to understand him and the
burdens that he bears,

When you've learned the fight he's making and
the troubles in his way,

Then you find that he is different than you
thought him yesterday.

You find his thoughts are sensible and there's
not so much to blame

In the man you lightly jeered at when you
only knew his name.

When next you start in sneering and your
phrases turn to blame,

Learn more of him you censure than his
business and his name,

For it's likely that acquaintance would your
prejudice dispel,

And you'd really come to like him if you
knew him very well.

When you get to know a fellow and you
understand his ways,

Then his faults won't matter, for you'll
find a lot to praise.

—ANON.

REAL LIVING

"A little more kindness,
A little less creed,
A little more giving,
A little less greed,
A little more smile,
A little less frown,
A little less kicking,
A man when he's down.
A little more 'we',
A little less 'I',
A little more laugh,
A little less cry,
A little more flowers
On the pathway of life,
And fewer on graves
At the end of the strife."

—ANONYMOUS

P. T. BARNUM'S BUSINESS RULES

1. Select the kind of business that suits your natural inclinations and temperament.
2. Let your pledged word ever be sacred.
3. Whatever you do, do with all your might.
4. Sobriety: Use no description of intoxicating liquors.
5. Let hope predominate, but be not too visionary.
6. Do not scatter your powers.
7. Engage proper employes.
8. Advertise your business. Do not hide your light under a bushel.
9. Avoid extravagance, and always live considerably within your income, if you can do so without absolute starvation.
10. Do not depend upon others.

—ANONYMOUS

FISHING A 'LA KING

Hol' dat line right dere, Missis,
Don move it up dis way.
Jes keep it steady—Like dat.
Put yo' han on de end of de pole
An hol it right dere—don move a inch.

Is you got a strike, Missis?
Wait 'til ah tells ya to jerk,
Give 'im slack—give 'im slack,
See which way he's goin.
Pull up de line,
Not dat much—give im slack,
Give im slack. Now jerk hard.
Ah Missis, not like dat.
You pull im too fast.
He's got de hook an all.
When ah tells ya to jerk,
Jes jerk—an hol' 'im right dere.
Don' try to pull 'im in.

Ah puts yo' line over 'ere.
See if we can git 'im yet.

Steady now, steady, slack
Yo' line—Pull up a bit,
Hol' im dere—right dere.
He's gone under dem bonnets.
Give 'im slack—Give 'im slack,
He aint dere now atall.
Pull up yo' line—Hits fouled.

We'll jus drift along 'ere
By dese bonnets, we oughta git one 'ere.

Ain't you got no strike, Suh?
Le's see yo' line.   Hits fouled.
We'll git ah big un in 'ere.
Yes, Suh, no man has to foller de advice
Uf nobody, less'n his own
Conscience says hits right.
Wot's de matter, Missis?

Feel anything on yo' line?
'Tain't nothin' but yo' minner.
Des 'ere live-boys, dey is.
Le' me put 'nother'n on yo' line, Suh,
Ah thinks he's daid.   Yeah, hits daid.

Put yo' line dere, Suh,
By dat holler log.   Now, Missis
Trail 'long dem bonnets.
We oughta git one 'ere.
Steady, Missis, steady.
Give 'im slack—Give 'im slack,
Don' drop yo' pole like dat,
Ya done scared 'im 'way.
Le's see yo' line—Yeah, hits fouled.

Naw, Suh, 'tain't dinner time yet.
Ya gotta ketch one, Suh.
De Missis, she done got one.
But dat'n aw'ile ago,
Dat she pulled plum out de water
An' den pulled 'im in too fast.
He's de prettiest one yit,
He oughta not got 'way.
Ah sho is sorry 'bout dat'n.

Yas, Suh, he sho wuz pretty.
We jes gotta git one mo'.
Dey knows on de boat,
Whar de fish is comin' from.
Dey knows dat I'se Old Reliable.

(Much Later)
Naw, Suh, cain't stay 'ere no longer.
Hit's dinner time, ah reckon.
We done got two. De Missis got one
'N you got one. Naw, Suh,
Dey ain't gonna bite no mo'.
Whots de use, if dey strikin
Ya can't ketch 'em.

—ELEANOR V. WILLIAMSON

THE LAST

When she told her story—
The war lost its glory
And victory seemed kind of sour;
How her youngest son—
When the war was won,
Was killed at the very last hour.

She had given three
For France to be free—
She had given all that she had!
But she was not bitter—
Nor was she a quitter,
Though her heart was broken and sad.

She was helpless and old
In a world that is cold—
All alone she must carry her load;
But a thing isn't real
Unless you can feel,
Or have traveled the same weary road.

—GEORGE P. HURST

TOYS

My little son, who look'd from thoughtful eyes
And mov'd and spoke in quiet grown-up wise,
Having my law the seventh time disobey'd,
I struck him, and dismiss'd
With hard words and unkiss'd,
His mother, who was patient, being dead.
Then, fearing lest his grief should hinder sleep,
I visited his bed, but found him slumbering deep
With darken'd eyelids, and their lashes yet
From his late sobbing wet.
And I with moan,
Kissing away his tears, left others of my own;
For, on a table drawn beside his head,
He had put within his reach,
A box of counters and a red-vein'd stone,
A piece of glass abrased by the beach,
And six or seven shells,
A bottle with bluebells
And two French copper coins, ranged there
With careful art,
To comfort his sad heart.

So, when that night I pray'd
To God, I wept and said;
"Ah, when at last we lie with tranced breath,
Not vexing Thee in death,
And Thou rememberest of what toys
We make our joys,
How weakly understood
Thy great commanded good,
Then, fatherly not less
Than I whom Thou has moulded from the clay,
Thou'lt leave Thy wrath, and say,
I will be sorry for their childishness."

—ANONYMOUS

IT CAN BE DONE

Somebody said that it couldn't be done,
    But he, with a chuckle, replied,
That "maybe it couldn't", but he wouldn't be one
    Who would say so till he'd tried.
So he buckled right in with the trace of a grin
    On his face.   If he worried, he hid it.
He started to sing as he tackled the thing
    That couldn't be done, and he did it.

Somebody scoffed: "Oh! you'll never do that"
    At least, no one ever has done it;
But he took off his coat, and he took off his hat
    And the first thing we knew he'd begun it,
With the lift of his chin, and a bit of a grin,
    Without any doubting or quiddit:
He started to sing as he tackled the thing
    That couldn't be done, and he did it.

There are thousands to tell you it couldn't be done,
    There are thousands to prophesy failure;
There are thousands to point out to you one by one
    The dangers that wait to assail you;
But just buckle in, with a bit of a grin,
    Then take off your coat and go to it;
Just start in to sing as you tackle the thing
    That "cannot be done", and you'll do it.

—ANON.

THE OTHER FELLOW'S DOOR

There was a little timid knock on our office door. We opened it, and there stood a man of eighty odd years of age, one of the finest, sweetest souls that God ever made, a man we had known for years, but in the hurry rush of our business and because he was on the shelf, we had lost track of him. As a matter of fact, we had neglected him.

He took the chair we offered him and the tears came into his old eyes as he said, "I just had to look you up. I don't get out very much; most of my old friends have died and, of course, the younger ones like yourself are busy; but this morning, as I came down the street, as I looked at men who looked at me and then passed on without even a nod, I was so hungry to see a familiar face and hear a familiar voice that I just had to look you up. But I won't bother you, I know you are a busy man and—"

The old gentleman tottered to his feet; we gently pushed him back in the chair. We kept him as long as he would stay, and as he left we told him we were going to drop in at his home for a good long visit.

We fully intend to, but business piled up on us, and this morning we heard that this good old soul had taken the long trail. Now we are full of regrets. Do we business men get so absorbed in our business that we fail to rap at the other fellow's door occasionally? We think so.

—ANONYMOUS

DAREST THOU NOW O SOUL

Darest thou now O soul,
Walk out with me toward the unknown region,
Where neither ground is for the feet nor any path to follow?

No map there, nor guide,
Nor voice sounding, nor touch of human hand,
Nor face with blooming flesh, nor lips, nor eyes, are in that land.

I know it not O soul,
Nor dost thou, all is blank before us,
All waits undream'd of in that region, that inaccessible land.

Till when the ties loosen,
All but the ties eternal, Time and Space,
Nor darkness, gravitation, sense nor any bounds bounding us.

Then we burst forth, we float,
In Time and Space O Soul, prepared for them,
Equal, equipt at last (O joy! O fruit of all!) them to fulfill O soul.

—WALT WHITMAN

MY NURSE

A cap, a bib, an apron white
  A waist of Quaker blue;
A smile, a curl, a face so bright—
  I like her—wouldn't you?

A gentle touch, appearance neat,
  Her heart—it must be true;
And all the while so very sweet—
  I like her—wouldn't you?

—JAMES E. WAGNER

A CREED

Man, adorn thyself with virtue,
Let simplicity be thy guide,
Let thy staff be staunchest courage,
Wear thy robe with kindness dyed;
By thy conduct prove thy manhood,
Wrongs avenge by doing right,
Banish from thy thoughts all hatred,
Defend truth with all thy might;
Stay cruel words and let not anger
Make thy hand some brother smite;
Should misfortune e'er betide thee,
The Golden Rule will win the fight.

—SHERWOOD P. SNYDER

TO A JESTER

I've played my part,
    I was glad to give—
For the spirit of giving
    Helped me to live.

—KENNETH SAUNDERS

A man may cry Church! Church! at every word,
    With no more piety than other people;
A daw's not reckoned a religious bird,
    Because it keeps a cawing from a steeple.

—THOMAS HOOD

CHRISTMAS EASE

If Christmas brought me nothing more,
Than a cozy chair by the open fire,
With the children playing upon the floor,
And I with a book and a well filled briar,
Or a friend or two, just to chat awhile,
And watch the little folks at play,
Recalling, too, with a tender smile,
The joys of a bygone Christmas Day;
If I had nothing more than this,
'Twould be a day of peaceful bliss—
Enough, I think, to more than fill
Most any soul with God's Good Will.

But Christmas joys spring not alone
From selfish comforts such as these,
And man can scarce enjoy his own,
Till he has done his best to ease
The grief and pain that, everywhere,
Abides among us, so today,
My book and pipe and easy chair,
Must wait till in my humble way,
I do the things I find to do,
To make folks happy round about,
And do them all so quiet too,
That other folks won't find it out.

Then when I've finished for the day,
I while a few more hours away,
And send a verse of Christmas cheer,
To many friends, both far and near,
And wish them all, including you,
A very MERRY CHRISTMAS too.

—C. A. SNODGRASS

TRIBUTE TO THE OLD-FASHIONED WAGONER

Back in the fifties when the old plank road stood
Which spanned the distance from Fayetteville westward,
Here once the veteran wagoner moved
With his products to market in barter of goods.

Many a four-wheel narrow tire
Drawn by two large horses have come from afar
With a heavy load o'er the old plank road
To the trader's town of fame.

With their folk-lore jokes around the camp fire,
Their bacon they fried in the open air,
And many an hour was thus happily spent
On their two weeks' journey, when to Fayetteville they
    went.

In that day the old camp ground
Was a favorite spot which the wagoner found;
There were no strangers along each fall,
For all were members of the wagoners' brawl.

One wagon loaded with cotton, another with corn,
Some carried dried fruits they cured in the sun;
And often four steady horses drew
A wagon loaded with corn liquor, too.

In the motley crowd that on this road moved
All were happy and all were good,
The standard of ethics to them unknown
To which we so often refer with a groan.

They were honest at heart with their fellow man,
There were none to defraud with that object and aim;
They were rough in hew and rugged in form
But faithful to duty and weathered each storm.

Life was real, for each day they lived
Time was no object, nor the hours with duties filled;

Each with a care-free life spent
Were gathered to their fathers in great lament.

Then with the passing of the wagoner
Went the passing of the road, few are now living
Who these facts know, for the road like the wagoner
Has served its day and they beneath the sod are now
   buried away.

—B. B. FARLOW

Dear Friend:

Have just learned of your great sorrow. My heart goes out
in deepest sympathy and love to you and family.

When sorrow comes or shadows fall,
The helpful word is hard to say,
But may God send his grace to lift,
The burden from your heart today.

It is hard to see God's hand in the dark, but if we wait
trustingly, he will show us and we shall understand.

YOUR FRIEND,

THE HUMAN HEART

There's a heap o' love in the human heart
   If we just dig down a bit;
It's the masterpiece of the Mighty Hand
   And He gave His best to it.
There's a heap o' good in the most of men,
   Just underneath the skin,
And much would show that we never know,
   Could we only look within.

There's a lot inside that we never see,
   And perhaps we never know,
'Til fortunes turn and we're down and out,
   Or sickness strikes us low.
And the heart is right in the most of men,
   When the truth is really known,
And we often find that the heart is kind
   That we thought was cold as stone.

We sometimes tire of the road so rough
   And the hill that seems so steep,
And we sometimes feel that hope is gone,
   As we sit alone and weep;
And then when our faith is burning low
   And we lose our trust in men,
True friends appear with a word of cheer
   And the sun comes out again.

And so I claim that the heart of man
   Is about what it ought to be,
For it's made of goodness through and through,
   Could we look inside and see.
God made all things and He made them well,
   On the true and perfect plan,
But He did His best in the greatest test
   When He made the heart of man.

—FRANK CARLETON NELSON

RESOLUTIONS

Resolved, to live with all my might while I do live.

Resolved, never to lose one moment of time, but improve it in the most profitable way I possibly can.

Resolved, never to do anything which I should despise or think meanly of in another.

Resolved, never to do anything out of revenge.

Resolved, never to do anything which I should be afraid to do if it were the last hour of my life.

—JONATHAN EDWARDS

FISHING REASONS

Fish can be bought in the market place,
So it isn't the fish I'm after.
I want to get free from the care-drawn face,
And back to an honest laughter.
I want to get out where the skies are clear,
And rest by the river's brink.
I want to get out where the woods are green;
I want a few hours to think.

Oh, it isn't the fish I am greedy for—
It's the chatter and song of the birds,
And the talk of the trees that I've known before.
I am weary of selfish words.
I want to stretch out, just my soul and I,
In a place from strife afar,
And let a few care-filled hours pass by,
As I think of the things that are.

Oh, it isn't the fish that I go to get,
Though there's joy in the swishing line,
And a splendid thrill when my hook I set
And a small-mouth bass is mine.
But my soul seems cramped in the stilling air
That is heavy with talk of gain,
And I want to get out where the world is fair
And there isn't so much of pain.

Fish can be bought in the market place,
But I long for the running stream,
And I want to be free from the care-drawn face,
And the city of dreadful dreams,
I want to stretch out, just my soul and I,
On a sun-kissed river shore,
And be, as a few mad hours rush by,
The man that I am, once more.

—JAMES C. ESPY

―――――――

GET IT DONE

It isn't the job we intended to do
     Or the labor we've just begun,
That puts us right on the balance sheet.
     It's work we have really done.

Our credit is built upon things we do,
     Our debit on things we shirk,
The man who totals the biggest plus
     Is the man who completes his work.

Good intentions do not pay our bills,
     It is easy enough to plan;
To wish is the play of an office boy,
     To do is the work of a man.

—AUTHOR UNKNOWN

―――――――

Hard luck stories are rarely valued at more than a dime.

SOBER   SECOND   THOUGHTS

If you must write that spiteful letter,
    Though "Why?" you should inquire,
Don't post it till you're feeling better
    Then—put it in the fire.

—NIXON WATERMAN

———

"Never get too intimate
With your friends,
They may some day
Be your enemies;
Never be too hard
On your enemies,
They may some day
Be your friends."

—ANONYMOUS

———

Good name in man and woman, dear my lord,
Is the immediate jewel of their souls:
Who steals my purse steals trash: 'tis something, nothing;
'Twas mine, 'tis his, and has been slave to thousands;
But he that filches from me my good name,
Robs me of that which not enriches him,
And makes me poor indeed.

—SHAKESPEARE'S OTHELLO

THE CREMATION OF SAM McGEE

There are strange things done in the midnight sun
  By the men who moil for gold;
The Arctic trails have their secret tales
  That would make your blood run cold;
The Northern Lights have seen queer sights,
  But the queerest they ever did see
Was that night on the marge of Lake Lebarge
  I cremated Sam McGee.

Now Sam McGee was from Tennessee, where the cotton blooms
  and blows.
Why he left his home in the South to roam 'round the Pole, God
  only knows.
He was always cold, but the land of gold seemed to hold him like
  a spell;
Though he'd often say in his homely way that "he'd sooner live
  in hell."

On a Christmas Day we were mushing our way over the Dawson
  trail.
Talk of your cold! through the parka's fold it stabbed like a driven
  nail.
If our eyes we'd close, then the lashes froze till sometimes we
  couldn't see;
It wasn't much fun, but the only one to whimper was Sam McGee.

And that very night, as we lay packed tight in our robes beneath
  the snow,
And the dogs were fed, and the stars o'erhead were dancing heel
  and toe,
He turned to me, and "Cap," says he, "I'll cash in this trip, I
  guess;
And if I do, I'm asking that you won't refuse my last request."

Well, he seemed so low that I couldn't say no; then he says with a sort of moan:

"It's the cursed cold, and it's got right hold till I'm chilled clean through to the bone.

Yet 'tain't being dead—it's my awful dread of the icy grave that pains;

So I want you to swear that, foul or fair, you'll cremate my last remains."

A pal's last need is a thing to heed, so I swore I would not fail;

And we started on at the streak of dawn; but God! he looked ghastly pale.

He crouched on the sleigh, and he raved all day of his home in Tennessee;

And before nightfall a corpse was all that was left of Sam McGee.

There wasn't a breath in that land of death, and I hurried, horror-driven,

With a corpse half hid that I couldn't get rid, because of a promise given;

It was lashed to the sleigh, and it seemed to say: "You may tax your brawn and brains,

But you promised true, and it's up to you to cremate those last remains."

Now a promise made is a debt unpaid, and the trail has its own stern code.

In the days to come, though my lips were dumb, in my heart how I cursed that load.

In the long, long night, by the lone firelight, while the huskies, round in a ring,

Howled out their woes to the homeless snows—O God! how I loathed the thing.

And every day that quiet clay seemed to heavy and heavier grow;

And on I went, though the dogs were spent and the grub was getting low;

The trail was bad, and I felt half mad, but I swore I would not give in;

And I'd often sing to the hateful thing, and it hearkened with a grin.

Till I came to the marge of Lake Lebarge, and a derelict there lay;

It was jammed in the ice, but I saw in a trice it was called the "Alice May."

And I looked at it, and I thought a bit, and I looked at my frozen chum;

Then "Here," said I, with a sudden cry, "is my cre-ma-tor-eum."

Some planks I tore from the cabin floor, and I lit the boiler fire;

Some coal I found that was lying around, and I heaped the fuel higher;

The flames just soared, and the furnace roared—such a blaze you seldom see;

And I burrowed a hole in the glowing coal, and I stuffed in Sam McGee.

Then I made a hike, for I didn't like to hear him sizzle so;

And the heavens scowled, and the huskies howled, and the wind began to blow.

It was icy cold, but the hot sweat rolled down my cheeks, and I don't know why;

And the greasy smoke in an inky cloak went streaking down the sky.

I do not know how long in the snow I wrestled with grisly fear;
But the stars came out and they danced about ere again I ventured
near;
I was sick with dread, but I bravely said: "I'll just take a peep
inside.
I guess he's cooked, and it's time I looked"; . . . then the door I
opened wide.

And there sat Sam, looking cool and calm, in the heart of the furnace
roar;
And he wore a smile you could see a mile, and he said: "Please close
that door.
It's fine in here, but I greatly fear you'll let in the cold and storm—
Since I left Plumtree, down in Tennessee, it's the first time I've been
warm."

There are strange things done in the midnight sun
    By the men who moil for gold;
The Arctic trails have their secret tales
    That would make your blood run cold;
The Northern Lights have seen queer sights,
    But the queerest they ever did see
Was that night on the marge of Lake Lebarge
    I cremated Sam McGee.

—ROBERT SERVICE

INDEX

INDEX (Continued)

INDEX (Continued)

INDEX (Continued)

INDEX (Continued)

—T—

INDEX (Continued)